# RISING ABOVE A TOXIC WORKPLACE

## TAKING CARE of YOURSELF IN AN UNHEALTHY ENVIRONMENT

GARY CHAPMAN

PAUL WHITE

HAROLD MYRA



NORTHFIELD PUBLISHING
CHICAGO

*The stories in this book are factual, but many names and details have been changed to protect privacy.*

Edited by Elizabeth Cody Newenhuyse
Interior design: Design Corps
Cover design: Studio Gearbox
Cover image: Getty images / baona / #162248449
Gary Chapman photo: P. S. Photography
Paul White photo: Michael Bankston

Chapman, Gary D.
Rising above a toxic workplace : taking care of yourself in an unhealthy environment /
Gary D. Chapman, Paul White.
Pages cm
Includes bibliographical references.
ISBN 978-0-8024-0972-0
1. Job stress. 2. Work—psychological aspects. 3. Supervisors. 4. Employee motivation. 5. Psychology, Industrial. I. White, Paul E II. Title.
HF5548.85.C45 2014
650.1—dc23
2014016911

Paperback ISBN: 978-0-8024-1283-6

We hope you enjoy this book from Northfield Publishing. Our goal is to provide high-quality, thought-provoking books and products that connect truth to your real needs and challenges. For more information on other books and products written and produced from a truth perspective, go to www.moodypublishers.com or write to:

Northfield Publishing
820 N. LaSalle Boulevard
Chicago, IL 60610

3 5 7 9 10 8 6 4 2

*Printed in the United States of America*

# Praise for *Rising Above a Toxic Workplace*

***Rising Above a Toxic Workplace*** **will save you from hours and hours of venting about your job. Its pages are packed with fascinating anecdotes and actionable solutions for the modern worker.**

—**Devin Tomb,** Associate Lifestyle Editor, *SELF*—

**Here is clear and practical help for millions of Americans who are overworked and underappreciated, feeling trapped in a dead-end job with no way out. In *Rising Above a Toxic Workplace*, you'll discover options you didn't know you had for coping or quitting. A terrific read.**

—**Jack Modesett,** Partner, Vega Energy—

**Many people feel trapped in toxic work situations, are victims of humiliation and intimidation, or are starving for appreciation. *Rising Above a Toxic Workplace* not only tells stories of violence to the spirit, it points the way to overcoming and transforming, much as Oswald Chambers described health as "requiring sufficient vitality on the inside against things on the outside."**

—**Marshall Shelley,** Editor in chief, *Leadership Journal*—

***Rising Above a Toxic Workplace*** **is a must-read if you are working for a toxic manager or working in a toxic workplace. Gary Chapman, Paul White, and Harold Myra's real world examples will help you realize the "grass *can* be greener on the other side" and no one should put up with abuse in the workplace.**

—**Peter W. Hart,** Chief Executive Officer, Rideau Recognition Solutions—

**Silent toleration of toxicity creates intolerable chaos. Chapman, White, and Myra pull the curtains back and reveal the true cost of unworkable workplaces. In this well-researched book, these noted authors voice the nagging feeling of failure and fear we or those we love may experience. However, they don't leave us with hopelessness but provide a robust toolbox for assessment and action.**

—**Brenda A. Smith,** President /CEO, Breakfast with Fred Leadership Institute BWF Project, Inc.—

**At some point, we need to realize every workplace experiences some level of toxicity. Once we accept this fact, *Rising Above a Toxic Workplace* offers employees and leaders a path to build understanding of the root causes along with simple, easy-to-act-on thinking that can help to reduce and minimize negative outcomes. It's an easy read that every credible activist HR professional will want to share with his or her business clients.**

—**Joel Lamoreaux,** Organization Effectiveness Consultant, Deluxe, Corp.—

**A modern organization is too often unhealthy. Toxicity, despite attempts to stamp it out, continues to surface in new and unexpected places. In *Rising Above a Toxic Workplace* you will find realistic descriptions and illustrations identifying work cultures that generate frustration and anxiety. I especially appreciate the practical advice—and recommendations for alleviating the pain—to workers suffering the negative and productivity-sapping consequences of toxicity. I would advise both leaders and the general workforce to read this book; use it as a tool to help you decrease frustration and increase engagement in your workplace.**

—**Lester J. Hirst,** PhD, Change Effectiveness Manager, Compassion International—

**I love how the authors approach the toxic environment from different perspectives and situations. That helped me to make a strong connection as an employee as well as a leader. Any reader can walk away with solid, healthy advice whether he or she is steeped in a toxic environment or seeking to prevent one from arising. The references cited are also excellent resources for an ongoing personal development program. The impactful style of this book transforms it from being a "how to" book into more of a "how to be" book.**

—**Dan Agne,** Senior Manager, National Sales Training, SimplexGrinnel—

***Rising Above a Toxic Workplace* is a desperately needed book in this age of bullying and burnout in healthcare. The numerous stories of people who rose above their toxic situation help you realize you too can overcome. This isn't a Pollyanna approach, either. Real world Survival Strategies and Leadership Lessons in every chapter offer concrete action steps. Questions for Discussion lead to deeper insight.**

—**Kathy Schoonover-Shoffner,** PhD, RN, Nurses Christian Fellowship USA, Editor, *Journal of Christian Nursing*—

**Chapman, White, and Myra offer compassionate advice to anyone caught in a demeaning work environment. Their words of comfort are matched by their practical advice and their call for courage. They show, with relevant stories, how one can take steps to overcome challenges, even when faced with intimidation. There is wisdom here not just for the young person struggling to find a way in a tough economy but also for those supervisors who desire to create a workplace of integrity, empathy, and trust.**

—**Mark Sargent,** Provost, Westmont College, Santa Barbara, California—

*This book is dedicated to all who find themselves in difficult places to work.*

*May you find relief—and the ability and the courage to do what is best for you.*

# CONTENTS

# INTRODUCTION

CONFLICT, HURT AND ANGER, poor communication, lack of appreciation—for decades I have sought to help men and women deal with such issues in marriage. Today numerous individuals experience these same painful realities at work. A few years ago I teamed up with Dr. Paul White to write *The 5 Languages of Appreciation in the Workplace*. We have been extremely encouraged by the response to this book. We found that the emotional climate in work relationships can be greatly enhanced when people discover each other's primary appreciation language. However, as Paul did pilot projects before we wrote the book and has consulted with a wide variety of organizations since we published the book, we became aware of the destructive dysfunctions in so many organizations.

Countless employees suffer in toxic workplaces, and perhaps you are one of them. If not, you likely have friends or family who work in such poisonous environments. When I decided to team up with Dr. White and Harold Myra, who has also had decades of experience in the business world, we were all surprised at the number of stories we had heard through the years of the mistreatment of employees. My guess is that if you talk to your friends about this topic, you will find that many of them will also give you their personal experience of working in a poisonous culture.

One of the most painful accounts I heard came from a friend who had been teaching math in the public schools for eighteen years. He had a stellar record of taking underachieving children and bringing them up to above average standards. He invested hours providing free tutoring to children after school. His fellow teachers admired him. All was fine until a new principal arrived and he began to find fault with this teacher. His room appeared disorganized, his desk cluttered with papers. The principal gave him twenty-four hours to get his room and desk in order. He said that he had received complaints from parents about his teaching. Though when the teacher asked, "What complaints and what parents?" there was silence. Day after day the principal harassed the teacher by walking into his classroom, looking around, turning and walking out. He told the teacher on more than one occasion, "You do not have a future in this school."

This teacher sat in my office expressing extreme frustration that the principal was intruding into his efforts to help the children. "All I have ever wanted to do," he said, "is to help these children succeed in life. I have poured my life into the children, and now this principal is making my life miserable." This emotional harassment went on for three years until the principal was transferred to another school and life for the teacher returned to normal. Fellow teachers affirmed their colleague and said, "We are so glad that you stuck it out. The children need you so desperately." I have often wondered what would have happened if the principal had not been transferred.

Most of us spend much of our lives at work, and for many it's tough just going to work every day. Our concern in this book is to help those who have to deal with toxic bosses, or those who are ensnared in toxic organizations, and to provide insights, encouragement, and strategies for survival. We give real-life experiences to expose what's happening, and to show what some have done to cope, and how others have found ways to quit and move on.

At the same time, we recognize that there are lots of healthy workplaces with fine leaders, and in fact, we work with many of them. We devote a whole chapter to such organizations and profile just a few of the great bosses we heard described in our interviews.

Healthy workplaces grow from high mutual respect and sensitivity to others. They are created when employees and managers learn how to express appreciation for positive traits and kindly confront each other when they are concerned about the quality of work being done. All of us have the emotional need to feel appreciated by those with whom we work. Most of us are willing to admit that we are not perfect and always have room for improvement. We are willing to improve if those who supervise us are willing to show us a road that will make us more effective.

If you work in a toxic workplace, or have a friend that does, we hope this book will help you sort through your options and find release from the intense pressure that comes from working for an organization or a boss who devalues people and looks only at the bottom line. We believe that, while profitability is a necessity if a company is to survive, it is not to be the only concern of business leaders. Taking people where they are and helping them develop their potential often brings greater emotional satisfaction as well as financial profitability.

Working in a toxic environment day in, day out can be a deeply discouraging and draining experience. We hope that both the insights and real stories presented here will help you—or someone you care about—thrive amid today's workplace challenges.

—Gary Chapman, PhD

"Life is 10 percent what happens to me and 90 percent how I react to it."

John Maxwell

"Along with every conflict in the workplace come flags waving in the wind reading, 'Listen to me.' But often all the combatants in the room are simply reloading their verbal guns."

Gary Chapman

"A lack of connection between management and employees breeds distrust, cynicism, and apathy."

Paul White

# CHAPTER ONE

# THE RISE OF THE TOXIC WORKPLACE

## WHY SO MANY OF US ARE BREATHING POISONS AND HATING OUR JOBS

DO YOU WORK for a toxic boss? Does your workplace feel poisonous?

If so, you have lots of company, and maybe this book will help you survive.

On the other hand, if you've had fairly positive work experiences, you might be as surprised as we were when we asked friends, contacts, and extended family if they'd ever experienced a toxic boss or workplace. Many told us sobering, even terrible stories.

Like most people, we had heard of "the boss from hell," but we never imagined how many in our circles would right away describe experiences ranging from highly frustrating to humiliating and health-threatening.

Yet we should not have been surprised. According to Gallup, seven of ten US workers either are "going through the motions" or flat-out hate their jobs. But why?

In our wired, globalized world, disruptive events impact markets, technology, stability—and people, as we continually see in the news. This upheaval batters worker morale in everything from manufacturing to retail to IT, from schools and local government to hospitals and banks. Employees struggle with economic uncertainties, downsizing, and demands to do more with less. They—we—feel overworked, underpaid, insecure, and underappreciated.

Attitudes sink into cynicism. The blame game escalates.

One professional, looking worn and defeated, told us that "bickering, criticism, and lack of support" had spread their poison through a workplace she used to love going to. Now, she said, "The tension here is so thick that I hate going to work. Actually, right now, I hate my life."

When a workplace becomes toxic, its poison spreads beyond its walls and into the lives of its workers and their families. In contrast, positive organizations energize and inspire their workers. When forced to downsize, they try to soften reality's hard edges. Their leaders know organizations thrive when employees thrive.

Oddly, toxic and healthy workplace cultures often boast similar mission statements. Both types cite values such as integrity, respect for the individual, and commitment to excellence. The difference is, positive organizations find ways to put their stated values into action, but toxic cultures allow personal agendas and other priorities to crowd out what they declare in print. Two similar organizations with nearly identical values statements might be dramatically different.

That's what a young father named Bill experienced in three large companies in the same industry. He landed a job in company number one, totally green and grateful for a boss who patiently mentored him. Benefits were good and the atmosphere collegial. But then the company started outsourcing jobs to Costa Rica and months later announced it was moving out of state. Because of family obligations, Bill couldn't move, and for the next nine months the company would fly him to their new headquarters to train replacements. He was given glowing recommendations to use in a job search.

When company number two eventually hired him, Bill was unaware he would soon experience the triple whammy of two toxic bosses in a toxic culture. Here's how he described it:

> What a contrast to the first company! The drive for corporate profits was crushing the life out of employees. One day we received a message announcing record profits for the month and then, ironically, another demanding that all spending for office supplies and travel cease. I was at my computer before dawn to communicate with Europe and after a full day's work, back on at night with Asia. I was on salary and got no extra pay for the extreme hours, yet my grim workaholic bosses criticized me for taking a lunch break.
>
> The atmosphere was all about company rules and success. The break room had a big TV playing only company propaganda. No pictures were in the restrooms, only lists of rules such as: only three pens or pencils are allowed on your desk; only two photographs are allowed in your cubicle.
>
> As I tell this, it sounds exaggerated but it isn't. Two able associates were fired. Another with a wife and

"The company I left observed 'Appreciation Afternoon,' and it got canceled because of work pressures!"

kids walked out in the middle of the day, traumatized, never to come back. I wondered who would be fired next. The team of eight I started out with went down to my manager and me.

Handling a major account with no support staff, my workload tripled, but my bosses told me, "We've noticed you're not asking for more work." I guess it's because they didn't have anyone else to handle it, but never once did I hear a word of encouragement from them. Yet they warned me they had a file of all my mistakes.

After two terrible years I gained a lot of weight, feared for my health and my marriage, and felt trapped, unable to quit because I had a family to support. Yet the day came when I knew for my personal survival I had to quit. I called my brother and my pastor for moral support and gave notice.

Wonderfully, the same day a former colleague sent me a message about a job possibility! Soon I was reemployed in the same industry—and experienced another stark contrast. I went from toxic and miserable to warm and friendly. Now at work we talk and laugh together. We celebrate personal events and pitch in for each other. Our boss goes out of her way to offer hands-on help. She smiles as she comes up to a group and asks, "How are you guys doing? Anything I can do?" And she leaves at five o'clock, signaling to the rest of us we're not expected to put in seventy or eighty hours.

My new company has on its corporate calendar "Appreciation Week," when it shows genuine appreciation for employees. The company I left observed

> "Appreciation Afternoon," and it got canceled because of work pressures!
>
> Soon after joining my present company I Googled its employee satisfaction rating and saw my new company was rated very high. I also checked on the toxic company I had just quit and, sure enough, it was right at the bottom.
>
> Oh, how I wish I'd looked that up earlier.

Bill's experiences with these companies are similar to those of many we've interviewed—employees disillusioned and wounded in one workplace but encouraged and energized in another. Some organizations are wonderful places to work, while thousands of others are so dysfunctional its employees become discouraged and disrespected enough to walk out despite the consequences—or desperately wish they could.

Author/consultant Annie McKee gives this description: "Toxic or dissonant organizations are rife with conflict, fear, and anger. The environment causes people to have physiological responses as if they're in a fight-or-flight situation. Healthy people become ill. Immune systems are less effective. Colds, flu, and stress-related illnesses such as heart attacks are more common. When you walk into a toxic organization, you can actually feel that something is wrong. By contrast, in resonant organizations, people take fewer sick days and turnover is low. People smile, make jokes, talk openly, and help one another."

What's going on? Are today's toxic workplaces inevitable?

"LIFE IS DIFFICULT." That's how Scott Peck famously began his bestseller, *The Road Less Traveled*. And if life is difficult, the huge chunk of it called work is sometimes the most difficult of all.

Pulitzer Prize winner Studs Terkel in his oral history masterpiece, *Working*, reflects what he heard from scores of his interviewees: "This book, being about work, is, by its very nature, about violence—to the spirit as well as to the body. It is about ulcers as well as accidents, about shouting matches as well as fistfights, about nervous breakdowns. . . . It is, above all (or beneath all), about daily humiliations. To survive the day is triumph enough for the walking wounded among the great many of us."

Yet work is also a source of not only sustenance but personal achievement and meaning. We all need work, and we're all dependent on one another. Life is difficult and always has been, yet today's economic pressures, uncertainties, complexities, and social breakdowns generate endless reasons workplaces fail to encourage and empower their employees.

No one wants to tell the boss bad news, let alone tell him he's acting like a jerk.

Chief among them is failure of leadership, often by high achievers unaware or uncaring about their own limitations. The painful realities of toxic bosses are compounded by what researchers call "CEO disease." The term describes the obvious—no one wants to tell the boss bad news, let alone tell him he's acting like a jerk.

A manager named Ruth told us about her boss at a small company. "He had no management skills, and he was not about to listen to advice. He loved to use humiliation as a tool and provoked infighting among our staff. At any time, if there were three people in a room, they were talking about a fourth. It was a horrible place to work."

As consultant McKee pointed out, workers in such places develop health problems, and Ruth was no exception. "It was consuming me," she told us. "My blood pressure was up thirty points, I had acid reflux, and I'd be seeing my doctor every six to eight weeks. He told me I was doing long-term cellular damage to my body. I told myself, 'This is killing me,' yet I had no other job prospects."

We've been talking to many employees feeling similarly trapped. What should a worker do? Confront? Hunker down? Quit?

It took Ruth more than five years to extricate herself. She desperately needed her paycheck, so she kept enduring the abuse. A wise businessman from her church counseled her on how to ramp up her job search, but she couldn't do much, barely getting through her sixty-hour workweeks.

One day she had an epiphany. At work she was demeaned and treated as incompetent, but everywhere else she was highly valued—as a mother, a friend, a valued church leader, and a neighbor. "These both can't be true," she realized. "People I admire and respect value me. That's where the truth is."

But that didn't lessen what the workplace was doing to her. Her businessman friend asked, "Are you willing to move?" Ruth had good reasons not to, so she said no. However, a year later when he asked the same question, she said yes.

Although willing to go anywhere and work at almost anything, nothing came of her applications and networking, and her health continued to deteriorate. She knew she shouldn't quit till she had another job, but she asked us, "When do you say, 'This is killing me'? When do you simply quit? I knew I'd probably lose my house if I did, but I came to the point of realizing that was better than being dead! So after five and a half years of misery, I finally quit."

Afterward, all she found was some freelance work, and it took her six months to regain the energy to aggressively go after a new job. Happily, her networking eventually paid off and she found a position a thousand miles away that fit her experience and skills.

Ruth now lavishes praise on her new boss and new workplace. "I now feel valued and supported," she told us. "Every day it's a delight to go to work."

Still, she suffered for years. In today's job market, it isn't always easy to move on.

WHAT'S MADDENING about so many of the stories we heard were descriptions of highly educated, well-credentialed leaders poisoning their organizations. We were especially jarred by leaders trained in psychology and interpersonal relationships who used their skills to advance personal agendas.

A supervising social worker named Clayton told us of his first work experience fresh out of grad school. He had worked in several human services agencies with healthy levels of common purpose and mutual appreciation, but that wasn't true in his first job as a licensed professional.

When he met the director of the small agency, Clayton thought the older professional would help him learn the ropes. The four other clinicians welcomed him and he enthusiastically started preparing case studies for the weekly team review. But in the meeting, he noticed a lot of silence from his coworkers. When cases were presented, the director would rush to point out what the clinician missed.

Here's what happened to Clayton:

> The director was unreasonably harsh with the others, but when I first presented, he softened his criticism. He even said the more experienced clinicians could learn from the new guy. It felt weird to be held up this way since I was the newbie.

Days later I presented a case with an unclear diagnosis. I expected the team would engage and work together to ferret out the best approach. Instead, the director laid into me, asking if my credentials were legitimate and how could I call myself a counselor if I couldn't figure out a simple diagnosis? I was stunned and humiliated, wondering if I really was clueless. I'd never been so embarrassed.

"We all got used to thinking we were inept losers who didn't really deserve to be paid."

Over the next few days, each one of the other clinicians privately let me in on the truth. Despite the director's experience and knowledge, he taught through humiliation. They said it was simply a matter of time before I'd be his target again.

I was demoralized, but I stayed, thinking I was lucky to have the job since I wasn't very good at it. I accepted my role as another abused child in the family.

Since I didn't quit after he laid into me, the director had the green light to verbally attack me. Every meeting was painful. We all felt relief when we weren't the target, but felt terrible for the one who was. We all got used to thinking we were inept losers who didn't really deserve to be paid.

Looking back, I can't believe I stayed four years. I moved up to supervisor and program manager but dreaded going to work, knowing if not today then soon I'd be told what an idiot I was and asked how I could live with myself knowing I was a complete fraud.

Our damaged self-esteem kept us questioning our approaches with clients, unable to make healthy decisions while trapped in a toxic and abusive work environment. We felt hypocritical telling our clients to be in charge of their choices. I began to identify with the "wounded healer" archetype, but in a resentful and self-loathing way. Exhausted and demoralized, I finally hit the jobs listings.

When I left, I gradually felt the darkness in my life lift. I no longer came home after work to withdraw and escape—I came home with energy and gratitude. My new job, with a supportive and wise supervisor, made me realize the depth of the toxic environment I'd been in. I couldn't believe I hadn't seen how bad it was sooner! I determined that no matter what, I would never again subject myself to a work environment that made me feel bad about myself.

WE EXPECT COUNSELING centers with their commitments to healing and their high degree of training to be community oases. When those values are violated, it strikes us as very strange. Other organizations dealing with social breakdown and crime often hire less trained employees and sometimes the combustible fumes in the air explode. For instance, well qualified with a PhD and considerable experience, Diana just seven months ago became the new manager of a community's corrections division. She had no idea she'd have so much to clean up. A tragic event had led to two investigations and the department chief, a deputy chief, and a unit supervisor were forced to retire.

Here's what she told us:

> "Toxic" barely begins to describe my work environment. Misinformation, rumors, and gossip are making this time stressful for everyone. Despite weekly meetings to keep staff up-to-date and address rumors, the toxicity multiplied. A few vocal, disgruntled employees approached the media, wrote anonymous letters to the mayor, and keep spreading their negativity. Everyone feels the turmoil.
>
> Our chief will soon retire, and he recently placed six people in acting supervisory positions. They are excellent choices. Each has shown leadership qualities, positive attitudes, and a strong work ethic. Yet the toxic employees are complaining they were not selected and are running to HR.

"We have too much to do to allow the toxic naysayers to control the situation."

Diana's solution:

> This week I decided I've expended more than enough energy and time trying to appease them. Many good employees want to make our division a model for all community corrections agencies. We have too much work to do to allow the toxic naysayers to control the situation.
>
> I'm hopeful this roller-coaster ride will soon be over.

Diana is putting most of her efforts into positive initiatives and resourcing those who want to move forward. She's playing both defense and offense, empowering those who can bring about new realities, and she sees light ahead.

Yet some workplaces are so toxic, the roller-coaster ride seems endless and the sooner one can quit the better.

That was surely true of a businessman named Carlos. He told us at a previous job his two bosses would go overseas to raise a million dollars, and then they would come back to use half of it for their lifestyle of drugs, alcohol, and women. He once walked in on his boss and found him lining up cocaine on his desk. Of twenty employees, Carlos says he was the only one who hadn't slept with the receptionist. Talk about a dysfunctional workplace!

However, he couldn't immediately quit. How did Carlos survive? "I just did my job," he told us. "I'm task-oriented and engrossed myself in my checklist of what I had to do." As soon as he lined up other employment, he got out of there.

POISONOUS FUMES rise from many sources, including bureaucracies that frustrate and stifle. Along with that, workers have been telling us how hierarchy marginalizes them, with the promoted looking down on those left behind, and the credentialed lording it over the non-credentialed.

> "A smile or single word of appreciation would have made all the difference."

A workplace mediator named David described the situation in federal military projects. He told us that thousands of workers with similar experience and skills find themselves in hierarchical environments where your place in the hierarchy can immediately stigmatize you as an outcast. "Contractors experience it as a brutal industry, with musical chairs, in which you're paid a lot of money but you get no respect."

David describes the hierarchy as having three levels: the contractors are third-class, civilian employees second-class, and those still in uniform first-class. "The irony is they all have pretty much the same experience, dress alike, and think alike. Most of the guys have served together, they're veterans, but those up a level or two in the caste system call those at the bottom 'slimy contractors.'"

Coming in with the "wrong" credentials can marginalize employees in many workplaces. A young father named Ted earned a four-year master's degree and enjoyed a decade of success in his field, but he suddenly found himself unemployed. After months of desperate searching he found a job in a local school system as a "behavioral interventionist," supervising troubled teenagers.

The administration did little to train him and nothing to encourage him. Twice a student assaulted him, but no one cared or asked if he was okay. Though Ted was the only one spending entire days with the troubled students, he was never invited to evaluation meetings.

Ted told us, "I had always found my opinions sought and valued, but not there. Only teachers and administrators were valued, with the handful of us on staff treated as inferiors. The atmosphere was extremely negative, with constant talk about drinking, partying, and sleeping around. Invitations to the school events to boost employee morale went only to teachers and administrators. It was tough handling angry, troubled kids all day, but that didn't drain me nearly as much as being snubbed by the professionals who never said a cheerful word, let alone an encouraging one. A smile or a single word of appreciation would have made all the difference."

Ted worked just a year at the school and here's how he endured it: "I survived by spending time with three secretaries, who were in the same boat. They said cheerful things; their camaraderie and the positive atmosphere around them would revive my spirits. I learned that concentrating my mind on that one oasis of friendliness and constructive attitudes would get me through the day.

They had no idea how important their encouragements and positive attitudes were to me."

## SURVIVAL STRATEGIES

**LISTEN TO YOUR BODY.** Ruth decided her paycheck was not as important as her health. Bill gutted it out day after toxic day for two years, gaining weight, his energies depleted. He paid a steep price and is still trying to physically and mentally recover. When your body insistently complains, seriously consider all your options.

**GAIN PERSPECTIVE.** Seek out someone objective and wise. Share the full breadth of what's going on, and then listen for new ways of looking at what action steps you can take.

**FACE YOUR FEARS.** We all have them, and too often they lurk deep within, sapping our will and clouding our thoughts. Surface them, confront them, and ramp up courage by seeking resources that challenge and inspire you.

**STAND TALL.** Clayton was too inexperienced to know that letting his toxic boss demean him would give him a green light to humiliate him again. In the next chapter we'll see an employee firmly confront her boss when she realizes she may be his next victim. If common sense and your gut say your boss is way out of line, find a way to draw your own line in the sand.

## LEADERSHIP LESSONS

LIFE CAN BE BRUTALLY unfair, and that's surely true of toxic workplaces. Even if you get out quickly, the unfairness can keep eating at you and your wounds may keep festering.

It's no accident that much has been written about the power and necessity of forgiveness and acceptance. Coauthor Gary Chapman has counseled many clients who have struggled with the ways they've been mistreated. One woman he counseled for two years couldn't get past her painful experience in her company. She was a hard worker in one of America's largest manufacturing companies and had risen to management. All was well until she got a new supervisor. Then, although she had worked there for twenty-five years, she was fired. She told Gary this about her supervisor:

> I couldn't please her. No matter what I did, it was never enough. I would work late and come in early in order to meet deadlines, but always there was something missing. All of my colleagues saw it and expressed empathy for me.
>
> I tried talking with her and asking what I needed to do to improve. Her answers were never anything specific. She just didn't like me, and eventually she accused me of cheating the company. God knows, I was not guilty! I would never do anything like that. She had no evidence but was convinced. So, I was fired.

That's when she came to see Gary, and week after week he listened to her recount the same painful experiences of how she was mistreated. She once brought a former colleague with her who corroborated her story. Gary tried to help her process her pain and move on with her life, but she remained trapped in her resentment.

For the next twelve years she invested all of her energy in talking with attorney after attorney about suing the company. She finally found one who would take her case and for three years she invested her money in a futile effort to "make them pay" for what happened.

Gary summarizes her efforts this way: "She essentially wasted fifteen years of her life fighting a hopeless battle. This is a poor investment of one's life. How I wish she could have accepted the reality that the world is unfair and invested those fifteen years in doing something significant."

## QUESTIONS FOR DISCUSSION

- *Have you worked in a setting you experienced as toxic?*

- *If so, what about the workplace or relationships were unhealthy?*

- *What factors do you think should be considered to decide if it's time to leave an unhealthy work environment?*

"Nearly all men can stand adversity, but if you want to test a man's character, give him power."

Abraham Lincoln

"Rank does not confer privilege or give power. It imposes responsibility."

Peter Drucker

"Of the billionaires I have known, money just brings out the basic traits in them. If they were jerks before they had money, they are simply jerks with a billion dollars."

Warren Buffett

CHAPTER TWO

# THE MANY FACES OF THE TOXIC BOSS

CRUEL OR CLUELESS, TYRANNICAL OR SUBTLE, THEY FUEL WORKPLACE MISERY

WARREN BENNIS, author of more than thirty fine books on leadership, describes authentic leaders as "exquisitely attuned to their followers and feel their pain, their wants, their needs. Leaders are richly endowed with empathy."

Bennis captures a core characteristic of authentic leaders, and the exact opposite describes toxic ones. As we've interviewed employees, we find it disheartening that so many describe bosses without empathy poisoning organizations they're supposed to nurture. Toxic leaders come male or female, young or old, smooth or gruff. They're toxic for all sorts of reasons in all sorts of settings, and those who must work for them face difficult choices.

Here's what a woman named Anna told us of her experience as a young mother needing to earn income when her husband was out of work:

> Joe was the worst boss I ever had. In fact, he was downright mean. He owned a 200-bed nursing

home and ran it like a tyrant, terrorizing anyone who crossed him or failed to meet his exact demands.

One morning we arrived at work to find the receptionist's desk drawers dumped upside down with their contents sprawled all over her desk—and she had to handle visitors coming in any minute. Apparently she hadn't done things Joe's way. Another morning it was snowing outside and a woman in an old car had gotten stuck coming up the steep, winding driveway. Joe ran through the lobby screaming, "That woman gets her car out of there right now or she's fired!"

"I looked at him and said in a quiet but firm voice, 'If you ever yell at me like that, I'm out of here immediately.'"

For all kinds of reasons people would sue him, but he had lots of money and lots of lawyers and would always get off.

Joe would storm into managers' offices and yell at them. Once I heard him in a nearby office screaming at a woman who was soon crying. I felt vulnerable and wondered if I was next. My husband was out of work and I really needed the job, yet sometimes no matter what, a job can't be endured. I didn't know what I should do or say when he opened the door to come out. The woman behind him was in tears.

Anna faced the decision that confronts almost every employee with a toxic boss. Should she confront him, or ignore him and hope he wouldn't turn on her? Or should she just walk out and look for a different job? Each worker in a situation like hers must make a personal decision. Here's what Anna did:

By the time my boss walked out of the crying woman's office, I had thought through what I knew I had to say. As he neared my desk, I looked at him and said in a quiet but firm voice, "If you ever yell at me like that, I'm out of here immediately."

He just listened and then moved on.

My boss didn't fire me, and he never did yell at me. In fact, as time went on he taught me important office skills and eventually promoted me to be his assistant. His thinking was strange. He had a saying, "If a fish smells at the head, it smells at the tail." I couldn't believe it when he'd say that, because he meant if the head of a company stinks, the smell works its way down to the lowest-level employee. He was blind to the fact—obvious to everyone else—that he was describing his own stinky self.

At the time, I was having a spiritual crisis due to our family's dislocation and employment situation. But eventually I began experiencing a faith renewal, and part of it was my determination to not in any way pass on to others the nasty attitude of my boss. He had positioned me just outside his office as the next person in line at the stinky head.

I determined I would never pass on any of his evil odor. To at least some degree, I could make untrue that if the head stinks, the smell goes all the way down from person to person to the tail. In no way was I going to pass on any of his mean, controlling spirit for it to flow to all the nurses and clerical people and women with mops trying to get through another day.

> I never had another boss even remotely as mean as Joe. I was fortunate that for some reason he liked me, but I had my line set and was ready to walk if he stepped over it.

Anna made her choice, and it worked out for her. A year later her husband was settled in a new job and she was doing part-time work elsewhere. Crucial to her resilience and ability to thrive was her determination, no matter what the consequences, to draw a line and live by her own values.

Yet speaking up to toxic bosses doesn't always work out, and even when it does, it can involve lots of pain. Drawing that line in the sand can lead to rough jolts and losses of security and relationships.

Like Anna, a teacher named Claire observed her boss acting in a way that assaulted her personal values. She had been given the opportunity to teach in a private elementary school and thought it would be a place where colleagues and children would be treated with love and respect. Yet one day her principal's actions caused her to speak out.

Here is Claire's description of what happened:

> The day I started at the school, it didn't occur to me there might have been reasons so many of us were hired as new teachers. I didn't ask why so many had left.
>
> During the next year and a half, I loved teaching my seventh and eighth graders. They were responsive, wonderful students. The principal, on the other hand, had very set ideas about student priorities and was oblivious to many of the things going on in their lives.

The triggering event was the principal's scheduling a program the same weekend as the Super Bowl, not realizing the conflict she had set up.

I was in my classroom with my students when she came in and started confronting them about their not planning to attend the school program. She lit into them, pouring on layers of guilt for not doing the right thing. I was stunned. These kids did not in any way deserve that. Never before had I heard an adult use such demeaning language on children.

Afterward I went to her office and, trying to keep my voice steady and calm, explained the students were just following their parents' lead, going to the parties their families were planning. It wasn't their fault.

She didn't back off one bit. She declared she was the principal and that this was her school and things would be done her way.

Once again I was stunned. I don't know where it came from, but my words just tumbled out. "Well, then, you can run it without me. I don't think I can work for you anymore."

Later I wondered, Did I really say that? Did I mean it?

Yes, I did! I was shocked at myself, but I've learned that when someone ridicules what I really care about or demeans others, I have to trust my instincts and carefully say something.

I felt a deep loss at having to leave the children and my colleagues, who fully understood why I quit. By the end of the year, all but one of the teachers hired with me also left.

Claire's sense of loss and betrayal was painful, yet her outburst and decision to leave turned out well for her personally. She found a job teaching in a public school, and went on to get a master's in administration and eventually a PhD. She became a principal in the school district and for many years found the freedom to bring her deeply felt values to her students.

For some, quitting leads to new freedoms for growth and personal development.

*THE PETER PRINCIPLE* created such a buzz years ago that the phrase became part of business vocabulary. A tongue-in-cheek book, it nevertheless laid out in a fun way some disheartening facts. Its thesis held that workers keep getting promoted till they reach the level of their incompetence. Often individuals are promoted into positions of power without the skills to exercise power.

Typically an employee doesn't see a Peter Principle transformation actually happen, but a hospital worker named Melanie did. A surgical tech working in the operating room, she soon saw why it was such a bad idea to promote her colleague. Here is what she told us:

> On our surgical floor, we had a lot of coworkers who radiated doom and gloom, and they loved to gossip. Among the nurses and technicians, about half of us had a positive attitude and the other half put a negative spin on everything. Some of us talked about their dark attitudes and agreed among ourselves that we were not going to let the gripers drag us down.
>
> Brenda was one of the nurses in the negative group, yet she was also good to work with. Despite

her attitudes, she was energetic and capable, with a lively personality. She was an effective nurse.

As a colleague, we had gotten along fine, but then she became our boss. Now we had to deal not only with her trash talk, but she got ornery with us and sometimes even nasty. She had her problems. She would disappear for an hour midday, and we all knew she was meeting her married lover. She was losing our respect.

One thing I can't stand is to see someone mistreated. For some reason, maybe because of her personal issues, she would pick out one staff member and harass her. She would exclude her from things and just pick on her until eventually the woman would quit. This happened several times.

For me, that was much worse than her orneriness. That's what finally made me go to her and say, "Brenda, I will no longer risk my long-term health by working for you. I love my job here, and I like you as a person, but I can't respect you as a boss. I'm no longer going to sacrifice my life here."

My husband says Brenda has an evil streak. I don't know about that, but I do know she had no idea how to be a boss. One by one, all the positive staff members left that job. They found other work, and one of them became a vice president of the hospital.

WAS BRENDA "EVIL," or just one more example of the Peter Principle? That's the sort of question many wrestle with, for toxic workplaces are seldom like good-guy, bad-guy movies but more like documentaries about inner-city dysfunctions with their complex causes.

Max DePree for years led the legendary Herman Miller furniture company with its year-after-year examples of inspiring and empowering employees, with great results. In his book *Leadership Jazz* he cautions, "An organization's cultural harmony is fragile."

Fragile? DePree says organizational harmony is fragile in many ways and makes this intriguing assertion: "Believe it or not, one of a leader's chief concerns is the problem of betrayal. Many kinds of betrayals take place in organizations." He then describes common betrayals, but his emphasis is not on villains betraying innocent workers but entropy and external forces at work.

"Certain facets of a leader's character are fragile," he says and names as examples truth, patience, love, commitment, and consistency.

Ah, *character*. That's where those questions of good and evil arise. DePree mentions in this context an ancient, familiar tale. Two of the deadly sins, Envy and Greed, are walking together when an angel appears. The angel offers them anything they might ask for, with just one caveat: the other would receive twice as much of what the first requested.

Quickly, as was his nature, Greed asked Envy to choose first. Envy thought a while. What did he ask for? One blind eye!

In today's workplace, greed and envy are readily available to all. Toxic fumes can arise anywhere in a workplace culture.

Sometimes a leader may be well-intentioned but simply is clueless. That's what Kurt concluded. As a young college graduate in a social service agency, he oversaw volunteers providing advocacy for juveniles in the court system. Staff turnover in the four-person agency was high—the woman he replaced had stayed only two months.

Kurt was new and needed direction, feedback, and affirmation from the executive director, but she didn't supply that. Kurt described her as inattentive, rarely acknowledging others in the room. A physical illness exacerbated her lack of social skills. She had recently gone through a divorce and abusive relationship, but she told her staff, "When I'm here, I'm here for you and I leave my personal stuff at the door"—but she didn't. Frequently she was gone when reports had to be reviewed before a court session.

"In a staff meeting," Kurt told us, "she confronted my colleagues and me about the way we were using our time, making assumptions without checking the facts. That tipped me over the edge, and I resigned. I'm glad I'm out of there, and others are planning to leave, too. What amazed me the day I quit was how complimentary she was about me and my work. She just didn't get it."

Many workers endure clueless bosses with big personal problems, and they can be especially clueless about relationships. Like Kurt, an assistant named Camilla in a large company quit, and later she was amazed when her dysfunctional boss called her at home as if she were a best friend. Here is what Camilla told us:

> My supervisor was divorced and having an affair with the married CEO, so she felt protected. She pushed her work onto subordinates and sat in her office surfing the web, and then she would come out and distract me by chatting—but then get mad at me for not getting the work done.
>
> She excelled at blaming others. When I was new on the job, she had me collect a lot of data and put it into a presentation for the board of directors. I didn't know anything about the information—I'd just assembled the documents. Yet during her presentation, when a director pointed out an error, she called me and berated me in front of the trustees.

Because of her relationship with the CEO, other managers didn't like or respect her.

With me, she ran hot and cold. One day I thought she hated me and would fire me and the next she treated me like her best friend. She would say mean, personal things to me and when I applied for other jobs in the company, she blocked my attempts. I felt trapped, and I never talked back to her. Others felt the same tensions and undercurrent, and we supported each other.

I eventually concluded my boss was dysfunctional because her life was falling apart. Not long after I left the company, she was let go, and she found it hard to find employment. That's when she called me, and I could tell she considered me her friend and that my relationship was important to her.

I've had all sorts of bosses and all sorts of work environments. I've learned to make the best of each, to endure the difficult and enjoy the good.

"It's so unhealthy to bottle up my emotions, but I'm forced to keep my mouth shut."

Kurt's and Camilla's frustrations were mild contrasted with what others endure, and they along with Anna, Claire, and Melanie were all able to move on to better jobs. Yet others feel trapped under domineering bosses who make their lives miserable. Here is what we are hearing from Janelle, who has been working in her company for seven years but is demeaned and micromanaged:

Our company tells us our input is highly valued, yet when I make a suggestion about a problem, I'm

> labeled a complainer. When I'm with my boss and someone in a higher position appears, she rudely ignores me. Her attitude communicates I'm useless.
>
> I enjoy my work, and in my seven years here I've never made a mistake warranting her always looking over my shoulder. She asks me questions that make me feel like screaming that I'm not a complete idiot.
>
> It's so unhealthy to bottle up my emotions, but I'm forced to keep my mouth shut. If I say anything about how she makes me feel, she turns it back on me as having a problem. She is never the problem. She never apologizes or fully listens. She draws a conclusion, then attacks—and as the boss she can attack without repercussions. I have tried going up the chain of command and that has backfired on me.
>
> I'm now much less of an asset to the company than I could be. I keep my head down and for self-preservation just do my work with little conversation with anyone. Yet the irony is this: in my self-preservation, I'm actually destroying myself. In bottling up my unexpressed feelings, I'm making myself sick emotionally and physically.

Should Janelle quit? If she has other options, yes, and perhaps even if other options aren't apparent, as Bill did in the first chapter. Or maybe it will take time, as it did for Ruth. It's a tough, personal decision in each case, but when health is being significantly damaged, it's necessary to take some kind of bold action.

IT SURPRISED US to hear how often interviewees said they learned a lot from their toxic bosses. On reflection, we can see how that happens since it generally takes moxie to become a boss—in some cases the worst controllers and manipulators have high capacities. Personalities and workplaces are complex and, as Anna found with Joe the tyrant, working under a dysfunctional boss may present opportunities along with the grief.

Mitzi, a mid-level manager, learned a lot from her first boss. He was her father-in-law, a small business owner, with much to teach. He provided her with good opportunities, yet when Mitzi couldn't perform to his expectations, his frustrations would boil over. He would use cruel words to demean her, and she says about the experience, "It was all very humbling, yet also rewarding. I'd never work for him again. It would ruin the good feelings I have for him now."

Later she had a boss who in many ways was like her father-in-law: she would praise Mitzi for outstanding work on a project and later comment, "I could have hired an intern to do this." Goal-oriented, this boss saw herself as an expert in providing feedback to her employees, saying, "Feedback is a gift." Yet that feedback was vague, sweeping, and discouraging. For instance, she said, "While you were out on maternity leave, your customers felt they received better care from your coworkers than from you." She gave no specifics or counsel. Mitzi felt very vulnerable at this time, and her boss took advantage of that, choosing to be particularly cruel.

What did she do? A very wise thing: Mitzi sought the counsel of mentors. Here's what she heard:

*Feedback is a gift only when it comes from a person who has earned your trust.* That helped her realize her boss's feedback was flawed and to not allow it to be so destructive.

*Although your boss doesn't give constructive feedback, you can give it to your boss.* Mitzi confronted her about the missing specifics in statements and challenged her vague assumptions.

In addition, Mitzi found frank conversations with coworkers helpful. "They were going through the same experience, and hearing their stories made me feel less alone. And it made us a stronger team."

However, her conversations with HR were disappointing. "They got me nowhere! One of the biggest lessons I learned is they're not there to help or protect you from your mean boss. They're there to ensure the company doesn't get sued."

Fortunately, that's not always true, but sometimes pressures on HR from corporate policies and government regulations stifle their ability to help.

Mitzi took her mentors' advice and explained to her boss that her vague, cruel comments hit her as mean and ineffective. "They make me want to cry," she said, "and I am not a person who cries at work. That sort of feedback doesn't help me better myself or the team." Her boss listened and adjusted.

"In the end," Mitzi says, "she made me a stronger, more self-aware person. I developed more honest relationships with my coworkers and strengthened my friendship with my mentors. And I learned when giving others critical feedback, I need to first earn their trust and give them specifics in a constructive way."

That's the hope when speaking up, but the contrast between Mitzi's experience and Janelle's illustrates how differently bosses react to candor. Some listen and learn, but others—no matter how diplomatic the approach—react defensively. When that happens, Janelle is right about what it can do to psyche and body.

## SURVIVAL STRATEGIES

**KEEP BITTERNESS AT BAY.** When you carry heavy responsibilities, working for a toxic boss can make you not only angry (which may be useful "coinage" if wisely spent) but bitter in ways that can make you toxic, too. Find ways to nurture your inner reserves and gain perspective. Develop toughness, but resist embittered resentments. Don't let bad leadership start to sour yours.

**DIVERT THE DEADLY STREAM.** Take another tip from Anna, who was in a position to lessen the noxious stream flowing toward others. Maybe you, too, could in some ways lessen the toxicity or keep some of the poison from reaching others.

**RESIST RETALIATIONS.** Florence Nightingale advised a long time ago, "Do not engage in any paper wars." Today, beware of email wars—they can escalate your troubles.

**STAY POSITIVE.** Think about this quotation from David Sarnoff, an early broadcast pioneer: "Let us not paralyze our capacity for good by brooding over man's capacity for evil."

## LEADERSHIP LESSONS

THE PETER PRINCIPLE is especially pernicious when it describes a high achiever lacking integrity. Warren Buffett, with one of his cut-to-the-chase quips, describes his own experience:

> I look for three things in hiring people. The first is personal integrity, the second is intelligence, and the third is a high energy level. But, if you don't have the first, the other two will kill you.

Think about that! In some cases two out of three might be okay, but not when it comes to integrity. A lack of it mixed with brains and energy produces toxic leaders.

Caroline Rochon, an author and trainer in Canada, told us she'd had her "fair share of dealing with tyrant bosses," so we asked her how she had coped. Caroline said she learned to take responsibility for her well-being and would ask herself how she was contributing to the situation. She said it took years to understand four different ways of expressing ourselves:

"When I'd respond passively, I'd simply let my tyrant boss get his way, creating a negative impact on my physical and mental health.

"When I'd respond passive-aggressively, I'd complain to my colleagues, contributing to the poisonous environment, or I would simply quit.

"When I'd match my boss's aggressiveness and engage in a shouting match, I would add fuel to the fire and make things worse."

Those three responses are obviously in Caroline's what-not-to-do list. In contrast, she says this about her fourth option: "My biggest lesson is something I recently learned to do: becoming assertive in knowing my boundaries and values and communicating them calmly and clearly."

It can be difficult to be calm and clear with a brutal boss and to maintain emotional distance. To gain some of that clear-eyed calm and a bit of objectivity, we might consider some of the ways children grow up to become toxic. Causes are countless and complex, but Joe Cavanaugh's description of his childhood in his book *The Language of Blessing* struck us as in some ways representative.

> My father tried to be a good man, but he struggled with alcoholism and inappropriate anger. At times he felt such rage that he became physically abusive and demanded perfection. He also struggled with bipolar disorder. I have calculated that, by the time I left home at twenty, I had received over ten thousand

> statements of criticism from him and not a single word of affirmation.

That's a lot of criticism! Cavanaugh says his father believed praising a child would cause him to quit trying to improve, so he ladled out large doses of the opposite.

Many in his shoes would have turned toxic, but Cavanaugh learned something that turned him into a leader with great empathy for others. He learned he didn't have to please his father. He learned to receive blessings from God and approval from others, and he tells a little workplace tale that shows the power of affirming people.

His friend Mary sat at lunch with Betty, a coworker everyone avoided because she was cranky and unpleasant. As they ate their salads Mary thought about Betty's skills and diligence and decided to tell her how much she appreciated them. Betty started crying and said it had been a very long time since anyone had said anything kind to her.

Mary learned that Betty had it tough. In childhood she'd cared for her sick mother and now cared for her husband too ill to work. She felt overwhelmed and trapped. Mary's affirmations and her listening had a profound influence on her.

The truth is, there are lots of people like Betty, starving for a taste of affirmation and appreciation. In a toxic situation, it's easy to focus on what's poisoning or even paralyzing your energy and spirits, but helping others may aerate body and soul.

There's a very old story of three men, one of them injured, lost in a subzero blizzard. Desperate to survive, one of them left the other two, saying they would never make it helping the injured man. Later, the two who stayed together stumbled across the body of the man who had left them. The warmth of their bodies working together kept them alive, but the lone man had only the warmth of his own body.

We all need support, in the workplace and beyond it. When we both give and receive, we stand a much better chance of survival.

## QUESTIONS FOR DISCUSSION

- *When you think of a toxic boss, what characteristics come to mind?*
- *What do you think about the idea of giving constructive criticism to your boss?*
- *Can you visualize yourself standing up to a mean boss?*

"Effective leaders don't say 'I.' They don't think 'I.' They think 'we'; they think 'team.' They understand their job to be to make the team function. They accept responsibility, but 'we' gets the credit. This is what creates trust, what enables you to get the task done."

Peter F. Drucker

"Everyone has an invisible sign hanging from their neck saying 'Make Me Feel Important.' Never forget that when working with people."

Mary Kay Ash

"Successful leaders understand that not everyone feels appreciated in the same way they do."

Paul White

# CHAPTER THREE

# REALITY CHECK: GREAT PLACES TO WORK

## HOW DO YOU BUILD A POSITIVE CORPORATE CULTURE?

CONTRASTS SHARPEN awareness. A mud-splattered car beside one just through the carwash reveals what the filthy car could become. We see toxic organizations in their true colors when we contrast them with excellent companies.

For instance, Marcus told us about the differences between two of his workplaces. After high school he worked for a small electrical company where the other two workers were alcoholics, and the owner "cursed the employees from daylight to dark." He hated going to work and says if he hadn't found another job, he would have ended up abusing alcohol like the other employees.

In contrast, when Marcus met with the hiring committee of his current employer, the chairperson told him, "Our job is to make sure you succeed. If you are a success, we are a success." Marcus has for the past eleven years experienced what he calls "an amazing and supportive environment that promotes success."

Unfortunately, toxic organizations are the ones that most often make the news. Media constantly feed the public reports of greed and exploitation, resulting in people's belief that most executives are self-centered and unprincipled. Yet it's not at all hard to identify leaders of strong, positive cultures.

An executive named Craig who represents his company's products in several states told us he feels fortunate to work in an atmosphere of mutual trust, where employees are valued, listened to, and fairly compensated. The past several years, as market shifts and downturns created extreme pressures on his company, he was more appreciative than ever of its stability and integrity.

How did his company resist letting its beliefs slide so it could survive a cratering marketplace? Craig painted this picture for us:

> "When ethics get blurred and I say to my boss, 'I don't feel comfortable about this,' she'll back me up, even if it means losing a sale."

> It all starts with our CEO. He's aware 3,000 employees depend on him and our organization's living up to its stated values. We have the freedom to work "as best works for you." That's huge! We're told, "Find out what works based on your skill sets and go for it." I'm on the West Coast, and what works here for me and my teammates wouldn't work nearly as well in our offices in New England. Our leaders don't micromanage.
>
> The fact is, one of our vice presidents who did was let go last month. He was a micromanager at heart; yes, organized and in some ways an effective leader and a good guy, but he couldn't help himself from trying to control everything. For years our

> leaders helped him function, but eventually our commitments to give people freedom to grow and do things their way clashed with his micromanagement. The breaking point came when one of his best direct reports quit over it.
>
> Our leaders made the tough decision to let him go in a careful and compassionate way, but it's always painful. Yet it opens a place for someone who more naturally fits.
>
> It's all about our culture of trust. In sales, gray issues arise. Two-thirds of my work is selling the value of my company, so taking the high ground ultimately pays off because our customers trust us. When ethics get blurred and I say to my boss, "I don't feel comfortable about this," she'll back me up, even if it means losing a sale.
>
> Here's how important trust is to us. Our company has set up an ethics hotline, and if we see anything that crosses the line, we can call. But none of us have ever needed to use it.

Speaking of integrity and trust, we were talking with a college president about a young executive who was promoted to lead his organization but encountered resistance from its professional staff. The president observed, "He needs to read Stephen Covey's *The Speed of Trust*. Without his gaining trust, his leadership will always be questioned."

Covey's book asserts that "speed happens when people truly trust each other." He views trust as a "pragmatic, tangible, actionable asset you can create" and sees it as "the one thing that changes everything."

Craig told us he sees this on all levels of his company:

> We were told at our national conference, "We want you to achieve your dreams. We support you as a person. If you're fulfilled, we both benefit." One of my colleagues on his weekends recycles old skateboards, making tables out of them and selling them, and so long as he gets his job done, our company encourages him. But I know other companies that communicate, "We own you."
>
> I saw an illustration of that when I was chatting with the manager of a small company. He pointed to a key employee leaving to pursue her dream of medical school. He was angry and made bitter comments about her.
>
> "You should be happy for her," I told him.
>
> He reacted with something unprintable. All he could think of was his loss.
>
> I've never once read in all the management literature that controlling, drill-instructor approaches give higher results. Quite the opposite! We all get a sense from our CEO that people are genuinely more important than our stock value. He makes us feel part of his team. The average tenure in our company is twenty-four years.

GREAT WORKPLACES, toxic ones, and perhaps most in between—the range is vast, and fortunately there are many good ones. Each year *Fortune* magazine lists 100 "Best Companies to Work For," and greatplacetowork.com lists small to mid-sized organizations. Best Christian Workplaces releases its own yearly list. *Working Mother* magazine even breaks it down to the "Best Companies for Multicultural Women." Although the best organizations face the same challenges of disruptive market changes, societal discord, and numbing government mandates, they persist in pursuing best practices and at least attempt to treat employees with respect.

Of course, you can also find lists of "the worst companies to work for," described as "continuing to make workers miserable."

Books like Jim Collins's *Good to Great* and many others show the ways positive corporate values result in win-win. Some of the best books are written by effective leaders themselves. Bookstores and websites list hundreds of such resources, and some of us find them inspiring, practical, and instructive.

Yet it's fair to ask: With all these authors and leaders calling for high integrity, why do surveys show most people strongly distrust leaders in every field? In fact, why did this book you're reading about toxic workplaces need to be written? Do these leadership books selling in the millions get purchased but then ignored?

One answer is that those who need them most ignore them.

The good news is, plenty of fine leaders read the books, learn from the seminars, network among themselves, and lead healthy organizations. And all those principles and commitments do flow down to the people producing products and serving customers.

One of the most intriguing illustrations of this can be seen in one man's story of his experiences as a new employee at Starbucks. A washed-out executive with no prospects, in desperation he took a job there and ended up cleaning toilets. He wrote a book about his experiences titled, improbably, *How Starbucks Saved My Life*.

Really? That sounds overhyped. Yet we found the title pretty much matches his story.

Michael Gill grew up in high privilege as the son of wealthy New Yorkers, and after college he began work at J. Walter Thompson, then the world's largest ad agency. Working hard, showing up early and staying late at its New York office, he gained promotions early and often. When he became a creative director/executive vice president, his accounts included Ford, Christian Dior, IBM, and the United States Marine Corps. JWT had coined the iconic line "We're looking for a few good men," and in the war room of the Pentagon Gill made a presentation to the Joint Chiefs of Staff that won the recruiting account for the Department of Defense. He was loyal, worked long hours, was always ready to adjust his schedule for a client. One Christmas Day when his little kids had just unwrapped their presents, he got a call from Ford. He left his children in tears to fly to Detroit and shoot a commercial.

Then after twenty-five years, when a new owner took measures to increase the bottom line, he was let go.

Gill tried to make it as a consultant, but the work dried up and his life spiraled downward. He lost his wife and big house, and one day—in his Brooks Brothers pinstriped suit—he found himself broke, sitting in Starbucks, sipping a latte he couldn't afford. A young African American woman in a Starbucks uniform asked him if he wanted a job. Her name was Crystal, and she became his no-nonsense, this-is-how-we-do-it boss.

His story reads like a novel as he describes how Crystal as manager and other colleagues day after day implemented the Starbucks principles. What were they and how did they "save his life"? He unpacks all that in his story, with core values being teamwork and mutual respect.

The Starbucks ethos is also unpacked by its leaders. Founder Howard Schultz has been widely covered by media and has written his own books, including *Onward: How Starbucks Fought for Its Life without Losing Its Soul.*

Now that's a relevant title! The competing themes of survival versus soul capture the twin challenges organizations face. With constant upheavals and disruptions, fighting for survival is a given, and in the threatening maelstroms, values are often ignored. Schultz sets his bar high to fight the good fight. He and his colleagues emphasize people must come first. They reject lesser companies' short-term thinking by insisting hard times require doing the most for workers and that you can't "retreat into success." Hard times require "doubling down on taking care of people."

In an organization as large as Starbucks, surely there are employees with gripes and personal hurts. But we see in Gill's experiences that top leaders' passionate concerns do flow down to managers and the workers serving customers. Starbucks founder Schultz talks about a great business being a business with a conscience and insists that "one can do well by doing good."

Consider that! Belief or rejection of Schultz's assertion just may be the dividing line between organizations determined to empower and contribute, contrasted with those that exploit employees, make the bottom line supreme, and ultimately exploit society.

WHAT'S IT TAKE to lead a highly effective organization? An MBA is not required. The following story from an executive named Kevin illustrates how an "ordinary guy" with strong character and authentic concern for his team members can create a place where people thrive and the important things get done.

> Early in my career I joined a company led by a dynamic man with little formal education. John was a good listener, decisive, fun to be with, and a man of extreme integrity. He didn't need "The Ten Commandments of Good Leadership" posted on his wall. He just naturally lived them.

When we traveled together, I never felt I was with "The Boss." Instead, I was working beside someone who shared my values. He inspired my coworkers and me to be the best we could be. He didn't fear criticism and, in fact, welcomed input on his leadership.

One time on the road we were discussing a negative situation with an employee and he said, "If Steve isn't having fun doing his job, maybe he isn't meant to be part of our team. Without fun, work leads to boredom and negativity."

That struck a chord. As I progressed and became a vice president, I always looked for ways to introduce a little fun to defuse a bad situation or help us through tough times. I considered it a good use of company time and money to build our team through fun activities, going to a ball game together or just sitting around talking. I tried to treat everyone as an equal colleague, as John always treated me.

We all benefited from his leadership. With the whole company working together, we experienced an eight-time sales increase in ten years. Not too shabby!

We could describe many more good and great workplaces and leaders, but perhaps the realistic way to conclude this chapter is to again point out that work often is difficult, and that's true even in the best of places. Considering the realities of human nature, we often react to slights or frustrations negatively. To respond positively takes the will to do so.

Hannah works in a chiropractic office in an atmosphere she describes as warm, welcoming, and a wonderful place to work.

But she admits it's all too easy to allow negative attitudes to creep in. Patients' demands irritate her. Difficult personalities sour her day, and sometimes she hates to see them coming in the door for treatment.

When she told us the way she changed that, she had a smile on her face:

> One of my regular patients annoyed me no end. He was like a lump of clay, never doing anything. I'd ask, "Did you visit your sister in Chicago?" No, he hadn't. I'd say, "You've gotta do something," but he wouldn't.
>
> I knew my attitude toward him and several others had to change, and my daddy's advice came to mind. When I was growing up on our farm and complained about the oddness of Stanley, our hired man, he told me you can always find something positive about a person—even Stanley.
>
> But what could I find positive about this irritating patient?
>
> As silly as it sounds, this thought came to me: He's got a really nice nose.
>
> I grin as I tell that, and truth is, it became a joke at the office—he's the guy with the nice nose. But he grew on me. He was an observer and asked interesting questions. He had no life, but that was his choice. I learned to enjoy him.
>
> Though I cultivate positive attitudes, griping comes naturally, and I get really upset when someone does something nasty or demeaning. That's when I say to myself over and over, "Thank the Lord I'm not married to this person! I don't have to deal with this

person. I can go home to my real, happy life. Keeping a healthy attitude takes thought and willpower, but it makes my workdays a lot more pleasant."

## SURVIVAL STRATEGIES

**THRIVE ON CHANGE.** As we try to cope with changes disrupting what we most care about, many of us tire of that mantra. Yet the relentless acceleration of change requires flexibility, whatever our skills and roles. We are hurtling into the future, and the future will soon be very different. Like an immigrant to a land with foreign customs and languages, we must continually adapt and cultivate mindsets that maintain both our integrity and capacity to contribute.

**DON'T GET BLINDSIDED.** In a good workplace, do you really need survival strategies? Yes! Boards and bosses change, roles and relationships are disrupted, and there's always an annoying teammate who messes up and blames you. Oswald Chambers stated what he called an open fact: "Life without war is impossible." He described health as "requiring sufficient vitality on the inside against things on the outside." Just as our bodies fight off germs, throughout life we deal with all sorts of "deadlies." Chambers said we must nurture spiritual strength to "score off the things that come against us"—an interesting way to think of our responding with vitality to unexpected attacks or reversals.

**STAY ALERT.** You'll find chapter 7—"Descent to the Dark Side"—details a surprisingly common phenomenon among good and even great workplaces. Sometimes it happens fast. For instance, a friend we knew built a multibillion-dollar conglomerate and then passed his CEO title on to his son, who promptly fired scores of his dad's handpicked senior managers. The company's stock plummeted and its thousands of workers were caught up in the turmoil. Chaos can suddenly erupt in unlikely places, and those mentally and spiritually prepared best survive the storms.

**STARE JOBLESSNESS IN THE EYE.** Michael Gill in his Starbucks book insists the trauma of losing his job, devastating at the time, was ultimately the best thing that ever happened to him. Joblessness can be rough or even catastrophic, yet it happens. Whether you're in a workplace that's empowering or exploitive, summon courage and a readiness to view whatever happens as the next set of challenges and the next adventure.

## LEADERSHIP LESSONS

WHAT MAKES a great leader? Jim Collins looked at the research done for his bestseller *Good to Great* and was, in his word, shocked. He found the CEOs who had achieved "extraordinary results" were not ego-driven but self-effacing. They blended "extreme personal humility" with "fierce resolve," channeling ego needs from themselves onto the larger goal. Collins said during interviews they would say things like, "I don't think I can take much credit. We were blessed with marvelous people."

Collins' discovery was fresh in coauthor Harold Myra's mind when he mentioned to Billy Graham he wanted to write a book about the evangelist's leadership. Billy's response was strikingly similar to that of Collins' interviewees. He strongly deflected credit from himself to others and to his team.

Few think of Billy Graham as a CEO, but he opens his autobiography by referring to his heavy responsibilities as CEO of his organization. Many have judged Graham's leadership extraordinary indeed, keeping together his original team for more than a half century, with remarkable international results. In the book on his leadership Harold devoted a full chapter to "Redeeming the Ego," a core dynamic in Graham's effectiveness.

In contrast, Collins followed up *Good to Great* with *How the Mighty Fall.* What did his new research find most often started the downfalls of large corporations? The first step in their failures was what Collins describes as hubris and arrogance. With those, an organization can very quickly go downhill.

Are you part of a good or even great organization? Much of the magic may come from leaders' humility mixed with intensity, their egos in service to the cause. It may seem ironic that leaders in the best companies are humble men and women, yet humility in some ways is as core to great leadership as brains and energy.

That means when you're hiring someone, it's vital to find ways to match psychological and spiritual maturity with the position's requirements. A person with great skills may become a lousy leader—and your biggest headache!

If you're in a great company and leading with high effectiveness, much of it may come from the culture there. A study of IBM executives found that stars who left for other companies often failed to repeat their successes elsewhere. Humility simply reflects the reality of what one person can do. It frees leaders from false bravado, emphasizes the importance of others, and inspires and energizes teams.

## QUESTIONS FOR DISCUSSION

- *Do you think a leader has to be trustworthy to be effective? Why?*

- *Have you known or worked under a really solid leader? What characteristics had an impact on you?*

- *In what area do you want to grow to become a more effective leader (regardless of whether you are in a formal position of leadership)?*

"Trust is a fragile commodity. Know your code of conduct and the values you stand for. Remember: if you wouldn't want to explain it on '60 Minutes,' don't do it."

Terry Paulson

"The leader leads, and the boss drives."

Theodore Roosevelt

"Achieving great accomplishments doesn't matter much if everyone who helps you get there dies along the way."

Paul White

CHAPTER FOUR

# HIDDEN POISONS IN NONPROFITS AND CHURCHES

NASTY, DYSFUNCTIONAL STUFF CAN QUIETLY CORRUPT A FINE MISSION

NONPROFITS ARE FORMED to do good and churches are formed to minister to the congregation and help others. To the world around them, they project sweetness and light—but sometimes their employees experience quite the opposite.

To put this chapter in context, we hasten to say all three of us authoring this book have worked with many faith-based organizations and ministry leaders. With rare exceptions, they command our high respect. We've seen many sad, sticky situations, but most frequently we've been engaged with churches and nonprofits with authentic servant leadership and personal integrity.

At the same time, the realities of the human condition make unsurprising the dysfunctions found in ministries. Like other organizations, they are run by all sorts of people—in other words, people who are human. A few are scoundrels who knowingly scam and exploit the sincere beliefs of adherents and staff members. More often it's the usual incompetence and Peter Principle at work, or high-capacity leaders struggling with their insecurities, weaknesses, or mixed motives.

Whatever the causes, the dysfunctions include many forms of deception to keep them hidden from constituencies. Appeals to "the cause" create pressures to conform to unhealthy codes. Poisons in ministry cultures range from subtle fumes that slowly sicken to flames that scorch. Some workers suffer quietly for years while others get fired.

We discussed all this with Lee, one-time administrative pastor of a megachurch with a toxic work environment. Here's the picture he painted:

> Our leader was highly egocentric and narcissistic. He controlled and micromanaged, and all information had to flow through him. We were expected to say the right things with the right language, spinning the truth and acting healthy when we weren't. More energy was devoted to creating and maintaining the image than to solving problems and creating positive realities.
>
> My boss disguised his controlling me by sending "I-care-about-you" messages. When he knew I was close to the breaking point, he would stop by and say something positive to keep me engaged. I saw him grooming younger leaders to make them receptive to his methods of control. Yet it wasn't all nuanced control. He would say things like, "You're an idiot!" or demand, "You call him and tell him how stupid he is."
>
> The disconnect between the reality of the situation and the image portrayed was huge.

Another pastor now leading a small, healthy congregation once served in a large church with similar top-leadership problems. Steve is trained in both theology and as a therapist, and as he told us his story, he was open and objective. He is not an angry person, yet he had every reason to be furious about the way he was treated.

The big church he served had been hard hit by financial troubles, so it had called a new senior pastor who found ways to solve its money problems. That gave the new leader credibility with the congregation and board of elders—but not with the large staff having to work under him. All the positive things proclaimed in Sunday sermons didn't filter down to Steve. Here's what he told us:

> Another team member and I were charged with leading the worship service, but we could never get constructive feedback. If we did something wrong, there was silence. We were left on our own.
>
> Once we were all asked to list our responsibilities and estimated hours. My duties totaled seventy or eighty, but there was no feedback except "get it done." When we brought problems to the executive pastor, he would say he would take it up with the senior pastor, who rarely got back to us. He used guilt to motivate, intent on controlling everything in the church.
>
> Twice in staff meetings the senior pastor said about declining membership, "I've been thinking long and hard about this, and I know the problem isn't me." In other words, the failure to grow was the staff's fault. We constantly dealt with passive-aggressive leadership, one week being told everything was

fine and the next that things were not going well and we needed to do things differently.

All of us on the staff were viewed as there to take care of the two leaders. They could ask anything of us, but they took all the credit. You had to sell your soul to function. They emphasized we needed to be willing to fall on our swords to keep the organization going, and we were expected to bend the truth.

"My executive pastor said, 'If people leave the faith over this, it's on you.'"

In our religious/theological atmosphere, that generated an added level of shame.

Some days I could barely function. I began looking for a new position and contacted a senior pastor who asked me just four questions. After hearing my answers he said, "Man, you are in a horrible spot. You guys are going to step in it, and it will blow up in your face."

He was so right! I kept looking for other work, but my energies were low. I was frozen. I didn't know how to quit, but I knew how to get fired. A year and a half later, that's exactly what happened.

The day I left I had a painful and infuriating conversation with the executive pastor. He told me, "If people leave the faith over this, it's on you. You're arrogant." He put all the blame on me.

Steve knew that the church elders and his colleagues wouldn't agree with the accusations, yet hearing those judgments face-to-face was overwhelming. He had been living in "the horrible spot" for much too long and it had indeed blown up in his face. He arrived home demoralized.

Just then a good friend happened to stop by, saw his devastation, and asked what was up. Steve told him he'd been fired and quoted the things said to him.

His friend was well aware of what he had been going through, and Steve was surprised by his vigorous response:

> He looked me in the eye and told me forcefully, "You know that's baloney!"
>
> The shock of his certainty cut through my emotional haze. For me, it was a brilliant ray of clarity. We both knew I wasn't perfect, but I had to put those accusations in their place.
>
> Over time, I've gotten past the anger and have come to understand why those pastors acted as they did and the stress they were experiencing as isolated leaders. I see now how I was part of a system and was contributing to the dysfunctions. I should have spoken out, but I wasn't thinking clearly. I had fooled myself into thinking I could change things.
>
> Some well-meaning people in the congregation really cared about me and said so. Yet I see now that what I needed was someone to tell me, "We love you, but you really need to leave. You're dying here."

Steve found his mature friend's forceful clarity crucial to his regaining health. Studies show that people who identify mentors and then nurture those relationships are the ones who most often succeed in life and work. Wise mentors supply many advantages, including objectivity—vital for surviving toxic cultures.

We emphasize "wise," because not all persons with opinions have the gift of wisdom. In addition, some mentors are more takers than givers, and some simply use a relationship for their own purposes.

For instance, Randy, fresh out of college with a business degree, believed in the value of having a strong mentor. He found one who affirmed him as a young man with great potential. Yet for the next several years, Randy worked for him in a variety of struggling start-ups and eventually, broke and exhausted, he realized he was being used.

That said, a good mentor can provide essential insights and reference points. In our interviews and experiences, we've seen that those in toxic situations who have developed relationships with wise friends are more likely to act sooner rather than later. One of the rich opportunities in life is to enjoy the counsel of good-hearted, experienced people and to identify those relationships especially worth cultivating.

On this subject, an additional caution is needed. One study showed that most mentor/mentee relationships last only an average of seven years, and often they end on a sour note. We need the richness of many good counselors all through our lives and an attitude that nurtures them. That way, we may find the clarity and resilience we need when things go awry.

Steve eventually saw the pastors who had wounded him as having their own struggles. The healing process, especially after a ministry experience in which core values and personal worth are assaulted, may take a long time. Yet hope does spring eternal, and sometimes even reconciliation is possible.

An executive pastor named Jason had an experience much like those of Lee and Steve. In a large, vibrant church where he ministered, the senior pastor's self-centered leadership style pushed the staff over the edge. He and most of the other ministers resigned and attendance crumbled. Finally the senior pastor also resigned.

Jason told us, "It took a year or so before I was ready to reconcile with my former pastor, but when we did, it was one of the most rewarding things I've ever done. As I hugged him I said, 'We will probably never be together again this side of heaven, but I don't want either of us walking around the rest of our lives holding on to this bitterness and hurt.' I walked away amazed at his new level of humility and transparency. It was a very healing experience."

THE UNAVOIDABLE METAPHOR of the oft-noted frog in slowly heating water failing to jump out applies to so many of our interviewees. Bill in the first chapter thought he was signing up with a company like the one with the friendly, helpful bosses he had just left. Instead, he endured two long years of debilitating misery. Kurt put off setting his own boundaries. Melanie got out before it was too late, and Steve finally moved on to fruitful ministry. But a woman named Eva started working in a ministry she thought would be a wonderful place of service but ended up suffering for twenty long, depressing years.

Here is Eva's story:

> I thought I was starting my ideal job in a ministry. I was reliable, loyal, fiercely devoted, and took extreme pride in my work and role. But as time wore on, more and more good people left the organization. The egos I dealt with daily were worse than in my secular jobs, and I became severely disappointed.
>
> Because so many left, I had the most responsibility, working way beyond forty hours without addi-

tional pay. After all, it was ministry work, and it was expected!

"I am now in a wonderful, secular work environment, and I've never had it so good."

The leaders offered little encouragement but often-harsh criticism. Praise was generally followed by "but." At every opportunity, I was thrown under the bus, and why not? They figured I wasn't going anywhere. My self-esteem was shattered and I felt worthless. Years dragged on and on.

I persevered, but I noticed a change in my personality. I was dismayed my faith and trust in people were being compromised, and I had no joy. I knew there must be something better for me.

I kept my eyes and ears open. God heard my many prayers, and finally a door opened! It required relocation and leaving behind many friends, but it was the perfect opportunity.

I am now in a wonderful, secular work environment, and I've never had it so good. My coworkers are team players, and we're all on the same page. No one has more work than another, and all are appreciated and compensated fairly. My employers are kind and generous, and they go out of their way to make sure their employees are well cared for. As in any organization, we have our problems, but for me it's "heaven on earth." I look forward to going to work! And the best part is, people notice the difference. They tell me how happy I look now.

I had no idea my lack of joy had been so evident.

The young and inexperienced, like Eva when she first started in the ministry, are most easily blindsided by toxic leadership. At least at first, they seldom realize the extent to which they're being wounded, and their buy-ins to the unhealthy culture limit their ability to take positive action.

College senior Tony thought he had found the ideal internship in the youth programs of a large church. He arrived enthusiastic about ministry and working with kids, but it was evident right away something was wrong. The senior youth pastor didn't get along with his assistant and seemed to be trying to drive her out. The team had no sense of being on mission. Tony told us, "I became the youth pastor's ticket to having the summer off and was assigned irrelevant tasks. When I was chewed out like a frat boy for no good reason, the leader who should have defended me did nothing. The nine-month internship was devastating. I came home depressed, broke up with my girlfriend, and struggled with my faith. As a young man, I had no way to process the experience and was deeply confused."

Tony and his girlfriend eventually reconnected and married and he's now in a job he loves, but his "devastating" internship still stirs painful emotions. In hindsight, he says he should have fled the first week he was there.

In other ministry situations, deciding among hard choices is difficult. A young pastor and his wife came to coauthor Gary and shared with him their story of suffering at the hands of three deacons. He had been pastor for three years of a church in a small Southern town. The people had received them warmly and after the first year, the church began to grow. New people began to attend and there was excitement in the air.

However, six months before they came to Gary, the chairman of the deacon board and two other deacons told the pastor they thought it was time for him to go. He listened to them patiently and asked them why.

"Because we don't like the way things are going. The new people coming in do not 'fit' with our church."

The young pastor tried to explain the mission of the church, but they did not agree with his vision. For the past six months these three deacons had brought the issue to the entire board of deacons, and one other deacon joined them. The other three disagreed with them and affirmed the pastor.

Letters were written by the chairman asking the church to meet for a vote on whether the pastor should leave. The atmosphere in the church family was tense. What is a pastor to do in such an environment?

This pastor chose to resign, saying, "For me, it's the best option for the church, and for my family. I'm not going to put my children through a church fight." Gary sensed the heart of this pastor for the well-being of his children and affirmed his decision.

There is no "right" answer in such situations. Some pastors facing toxic leadership choose to resign. When this happens the church usually loses its newest members and goes back to being a small group of like-minded people, who make little impact on their community. If the pastor chooses to stay, he faces a series of battles with the opposition, ultimately ending with one or the other leaving. The church often loses its influence in the community.

A counselor named Ivan wasn't ambivalent about leaving his abusive nonprofit when he eventually understood the depth of its dysfunction. He served as one of a half-dozen program directors for a social service agency, and here is the tale he told us.

> Our autocratic leader demanded intense loyalty, no questions asked, and she had the power to do

whatever she pleased. She was untouchable, and her attitude was the mission justified whatever was done. She assumed the worst of employees. For instance, anyone—including clients—could lodge a complaint against you and without hearing your side, she'd accuse you in a group meeting.

Ethical problems were covered up. Each of our local programs had an advisory board, but we were forbidden to talk to them. The organization was full of deceit.

As I looked around at my colleagues, I realized the environment was making them physically and psychologically sick. To work there, you had to become dysfunctional.

For me it came to a head when a colleague was forced to quit. To save having to pay unemployment, the leader told the state he had quit for personal reasons. That was clearly unethical, and when I was asked by officials, I told them the truth. Not long after, the leader called me into her office. She sat me down and asked, "Are you happy working here?"

The truth was I loved my job, but I didn't like the person I was becoming. I couldn't allow myself to get dysfunctional like so many of my coworkers. Although I had two small children to support, I started writing my resume and six months later found another position.

Two weeks before I left I asked to see my personnel file. The director controlled those files, and I was shown only part of them. But a week before I left, the assistant director, whom I respected and who wanted to do the right thing, drove ninety minutes to

> our local office to give me a large packet, my complete file. I found in it that I was being set up to take the fall in a legal situation.

Apparently Ivan got out just in time. We asked him how he kept sane during his time there and he said he had a good support system in the local staff. Even in dysfunctional cultures, good relationships can be nurtured. He added he also had support in his church and met with friends for breakfast once a week.

When navigating choppy waters, connecting in positive ways with others becomes essential, and when possible, getting to a healthy place becomes the high priority.

IT'S FITTING WE END this chapter as we started it, with affirmation of the many empowering ministries we've been associated with—and a brief illustration, one of many we could share.

Wayne was in a ministry he loved, doing work he loved. But after a long track record of success and fulfillment, in a very short time he was hit by a double personal crisis. His wife was diagnosed with serious cancer, and his teenage son was hospitalized with a mental illness.

As he scrambled from crisis to crisis and tried week after week to navigate all the 24/7 demands, Wayne found his inner resources weakening. Everything was falling apart—even his job. At least that's how he felt, because his work was ministering to teenagers, so his son's troubles and substance abuse made him feel disqualified.

One day his boss stopped by and because they had known each other for years, Wayne confided his worries that his apparent ineffectiveness as a father made him feel his failures invalidated his work. His boss responded, "No way!" He affirmed his employee's excellent work, saying it wasn't at all negated by his son's troubles.

Wayne was an early riser, and so was the organization's president, who stopped by his office one morning before others arrived. He asked for an update on what his family was going through and he gave Wayne an inspirational book he'd found helpful in his own hard times.

Those encounters with the organization's top leaders helped him to continue working, parenting and staying steady through his wife's cancer treatments. Both of his leaders had simply come to him as caring colleagues. Wayne knew his son's illness didn't invalidate his ministry, but hearing his boss vigorously affirm that put his anxieties to rest. The book the president handed him became a rich resource for years to come.

His wife beat the cancer, his son is now employed and soon to be married, and Wayne is still doing the work he loves.

All of us in the workforce not only labor with our colleagues but live with a mixture of joys and hard things like cancer, tragic accidents, and trauma with our children. Life is difficult, and we all hit white water. When colleagues reach out and stated values are the natural reality, ministries become oases "for the common good."

## SURVIVAL STRATEGIES

**SEE THROUGH THE FOG.** Eva, Tony, and Ivan are perfect examples of needing to see clearly and to act early. So often workers have too few reference points to grasp what's happening to them, and far too often, circumstances keep them from standing up for themselves. Seek clarity about what's really going on, consult with your bases of support, and take carefully considered action.

**COMPARE "BEST PRACTICES."** If you're wondering if what happens in your workplace is simply what "comes with the territory," check out what's happening elsewhere. Network to get a picture of the chemistry and dynamics in similar organizations.

**GET TOUGH.** Mental and spiritual toughness go together. Deepen your commitment to your most essential values and mentally rehearse the specific ways you can take positive action. Read a book like *Stress for Success* or *Toughness Training for Life* by James Loehr.

## LEADERSHIP LESSONS

WORKING IN A PLACE that helps people, and hearing all the talk about the organization's good works, can dull awareness of dysfunctions. Few students are prepared for what they may face in their jobs—yet resources are readily available. For instance, *Leadership* journal has long brought to ministry workplaces a wealth of insights and stories unrelentingly real.

We went to the *Leadership* website and saw that its lead article was titled "Fired." It's the story of a young pastor named Nathan Kilgore who was let go from his church not from misconduct or ineffectiveness, but due to . . . his attitude.

Nathan now admits he didn't like the senior pastor's leadership style and that his attitude was toxic. Here's a case where the subordinate, not his leader, was poisoning the well. Nathan says,

"I dug my own grave," and adds, "I guess John Maxwell is right. Attitude is everything."

He also ruefully remembers his mother's posting on a wall: "It's better to remain silent and be thought a fool than to speak up and remove all doubt." He now realizes his thinking had to be seriously realigned.

Right after being fired, Nathan phoned a former professor to tell him what had happened and was taken aback by his response. The older man told him, "That's great!"

Nathan, stunned, asked, "What do you mean, that's great?"

"It sounds as if God is getting ready to do something really big in your life."

Well, it all depends on what one considers big. Nathan ended up for a year at low wages doing backbreaking work digging ditches. He learned raw and rugged lessons and a far deeper way of looking at vocation and attitude.

Reading such accounts gives us multiple ways to view our own circumstances. Sometimes they help us become aware of our own contributions to discord. Other times they help us realize we've bought into a sick culture that we can't change and we need to study exit strategies others have used.

And, happily, sometimes they make us grateful we're not experiencing all those betrayals, daily nastiness, and humiliations we read others are living through.

## QUESTIONS FOR DISCUSSION

- *Do you think toxicity displays itself differently in a non-profit organization in contrast to a business? If so, how?*

- *Do you have someone in your life who could be a mentor or advisor to you? What steps could you take to start meeting with someone?*

- *Do you now see that a past negative experience in your life provided an opportunity to grow and learn valuable lessons? If so, what did you learn?*

"You don't have to be crazy to work here. We'll train you."

Sign seen in a flower shop

"To those who value words of affirmation, criticism feels like a knife in the heart."

Paul White

"It takes time and conscious choice to listen."

Gary Chapman

## CHAPTER FIVE

# LITTLE MURDERS AT WORK

### WHEN WORDS CUT LIKE KNIVES AND SPITE SHATTERS THE PEACE

FILM CRITIC ROGER Ebert, reviewing the 1971 movie *Little Murders*, concluded, “It’s a very New York kind of movie, paranoid, masochistic and nervous. It left me with a cold knot in my stomach, a vague fear that something was gaining on me.”

Sometimes work can be like that, with deadly intent, with covert glances and whispers in corners. Words slice. Rejections wound. In the workplace the phrase “little murders” brings to mind slow destruction of the soul and spirit.

Of course, there are no *little* murders.

The late Henri Nouwen once observed, “Community is the place where the person you least want to live with always lives.” The same might be said of work.

From brief skirmishes to ongoing vendettas, conflict in workplaces can destroy organizations and poison the hearts and souls of leaders and those they lead. Sometimes hostilities flare from just one unfair criticism or a misunderstanding that grows into a destructive fire. After a hurtful incident, sometimes it's possible to find a way to douse the flames.

Amelia found that out. An engineer in her mid-twenties doing hardware design in a large company, she's the youngest on her team of eight. Her teammates are all married with kids or in long-term relationships, so she feels little in common with them. She likes and respects Carson, her boss who is in his late forties. She considered the other woman on her team, Nancy, as a mentor and had a positive relationship with her—until a bewildering event.

> I was called into a meeting with Carson, Nancy, and another teammate. After a few introductory remarks, Carson launched into a twenty-minute monologue critiquing my work. I was stunned. I had no idea this was coming. No one had ever voiced concerns about my work. Carson was berating me for taking on too much work and not meeting deadlines. He lectured me that I needed to set boundaries and complete my work on time.
>
> How could this be happening in a group meeting? Nancy and my other coworker were silent. I was hurt and embarrassed.
>
> That evening I emailed Carson and asked for time to talk to him the next day. Then I spent the night researching my work and found only two instances of missed deadlines—and those were six months before.

Amelia was relieved to learn from Carson that his concerns were actually Nancy's, who had told him she didn't know how to voice them to Amelia. He apologized for his inappropriate way of communicating and affirmed her work ethic and contributions to the team.

Fortunately for Amelia, her boss listened and made amends. Yet he had failed to live up to basic principles in several ways: He attempted indirect communication through him from Nancy to Amelia, he never verified Nancy's information, he confronted in front of team members, and instead of thoughtful questioning he delivered an emotionally charged monologue that to Amelia felt like a personal attack.

To her credit, Amelia didn't just curl up and lick her wounds—she asked for a meeting and dug into the data.

What about Nancy's concerns? Amelia plans to approach her, saying she is confused and wants to establish direct communications. In addition, she'll document and communicate to her team the projects she's working on and the progress she's making, and she'll ask Carson how he prefers to keep abreast of her work and progress. She also plans to stop saying "I can get it done" to every request.

So here we have an illustration of wise actions averting what could have become a backstabbing feud. However, it took an understanding boss willing to admit his mistake, and not every boss is like that.

A CPA named Eugene worked for a guy who would never admit to a mistake, and anyone pointing one out or simply disagreeing with him might not be around for long. Here's how he described his mercurial boss:

> He was a successful entrepreneur who had gone against common wisdom and built a thriving business. In the morning he'd come in with 400 ideas, but by evening he'd have just one left. He'd tell you some-

thing and later completely reverse his instructions. You could never make your own decisions.

Once he talked to us for twenty minutes about providing great customer service, and two days later he was upset because we had spent $50 keeping a customer happy. He would put someone in charge of his three stores, but no one could satisfy him and he would fire them.

That happened to me. He had given me responsibility for his stores, and that lasted three months because in a meeting I disagreed with him. "That's shortsighted," I told him. "You need to look at the big picture."

He didn't argue, but an hour later he was telling me I should go back to being a CPA, that I should open my own firm and he would be a client.

I asked him, "How long do I have here?"

He blew up. "I didn't say I was firing you!"

Fifteen minutes later he came back and said, "You have two weeks."

Bosses come with all sorts of backgrounds, personalities, and methods, and sometimes adapting stretches a person's limits. Motivators tell us, "Thrive on change," yet often change is traumatic and doesn't at all feel like a recipe for thriving. For instance, clashes between two strong leaders can present some hard choices, as in the following story:

Ross was a successful, creative leader in a Northeast packaging company. For the past dozen years he consistently grew his division at a profit, but unnoticed shortfalls in other divisions suddenly came to light and the company found itself awash in red ink. In response, a "crocodile" was hired. Ross knew that's what the new vice president was because his early questions zeroed in on which employees might be expendable.

Before long his new boss informed Ross that staff would be reduced throughout the company, and that included his division. Yet Ross's employees were making his division flourish and contribute hefty amounts of profit. Years before, he had recruited and trained them until they became an effective team at the peak of their productivity.

> "The man was a controller, a short guy in an expensive suit determined to loom over you."

The crocodile insisted that to be fair, cuts would be made across the organization.

One afternoon Ross asked, "How much profit do you need from my division? Why let people go when they're generating income? Give me a number. Tell me, and I'll deliver it."

He was told that wasn't the way it worked.

Ross's most recent hire was an older man who had just left a secure job to join them. Forced to fire him, Ross barely slept. His issues went far beyond staff reductions. Here's how he described his boss:

> The man was a controller, a short guy in an expensive suit determined to loom over you. Instead of setting people free to flourish, he saw them as pieces on his chessboard. He would smile at you, a hard

> brick under his velvet glove. There was no give and take, as I'd always had with my previous bosses.
>
> I wrote him a long memo detailing my concerns. He smoothly responded that if I felt that way, I should leave.
>
> That appalled me, not only for my sake but for all of us in the company. He was intent on completing his chess game, willfully blind to the fact my leaving would cause an exodus of our best people and a huge loss of money and momentum. His thinking reminded me of that defense of Vietnam War strategy: "We had to destroy the village in order to save it."
>
> I simply couldn't knuckle under to this guy. He violated all my principles about how to lead the people counting on me.
>
> One night I had a dream. I was on a train with my colleagues when terrorists attacked. My new boss was leading them, and he came at me. I grabbed his arm, twisted it, and rammed his shoulder down. Then I raised my fist to smash his elbow—but woke up, my heart pounding.
>
> I'd never before had a dream with such clear meaning. I could break my boss's arm since I had plenty of equity in the company. I could fight to get him fired, attacking him and his strategies with my team and allies. I knew how to use a brick as well as he did. But there would be lots of blood on the carpet.

Ross decided to leave without warfare. He was quickly hired as CEO of another company in the same industry and went on to build new outstanding teams. Many of his colleagues left and thrived elsewhere, but the company experienced significant losses from their departures.

Why didn't Ross "fight the good fight" so he could continue to lead his team and help his company stay true to its values? He told us, "Believe me, I was tempted. But I decided that's just what it was, temptation. I was getting lured into a crazy mixture of anger, despair, and vengeful ideas of how to expose him and some of the board members who were simply stupid about this guy. It took me a long time and lots of prayer to see all the implications of my actions one way or another. It stretched and deepened me and prepared me for new challenges, which turned out to be huge and wonderful."

Sometimes, with "righteous indignation," you decide to right a wrong, and sometimes you just walk away.

MURDER? MANY an employee, working under an unappreciative boss, may feel like committing it.

Susan, an educator at a large university, for thirteen years coordinated services for students with disabilities. She was highly qualified, served on search committees for new directors, and was responsible for much of the training. By studying and working hard she gained the academic credentials needed for promotion. The fourth time a director's position opened up, she declined the invitation to serve on the search committee and told her boss she intended to apply for the position.

For reasons known only to him he told her, "You will not get it."

Susan told us, "I knew he had the final say, and my fate was sealed. I was crushed."

Instead of becoming bitter, she maintained her momentum. "I began opening myself up to exploring other positions. I didn't let this episode poison my service or my attitude. That could have led to a toxic environment for everyone."

Exactly right! Susan was wise enough to see that if she reacted with anger and accusation, she would be affecting the entire department and beyond. And it must have been especially tempting to say something when the person chosen for the job came into her office, looked her in the eye, and said, "Susan, this job should be yours, and we all know it. You're the perfect person for it."

She did not let his comment supply ammunition for getting back at the boss. She didn't let the injustice seethe within. Instead she let the new director know she appreciated his saying that and would support him 100 percent. "I told him I'd help him get a hang of the office. I also told him that due to the VP's placing a limit on my upward mobility, I was looking for other positions."

Susan's job search resulted in being hired not in academia but in a corporate environment. She tells us, "I absolutely LOVE my new position."

We've found taking a hit and moving on is often better than attempts to undo unfairness or insist on one's rights—even when they're completely valid.

At an Eastern university a young professor did a great deal of research into a topic with his department head. It came as a nasty surprise when the senior professor announced he was publishing a book using material they had developed together, with no credit given to the younger man.

That his senior colleague would do that seemed outrageous and came as a crushing blow. He felt he should take strong action.

Wisely, the young professor asked a mentor to join him for lunch and they discussed what he should do. Although the older professor had violated common decency and, in a "publish-or-perish" environment, had acted unfairly, they agreed the situation would be viewed as ambiguous. The young professor was due rightful recognition, but demanding it would create waves of dissonance, not only between the professors but in the department and among students. They agreed the best plan was to not press the case but to move on to other projects.

The young professor went on to write numerous books and to receive significant recognition for his excellence in teaching and scholarship.

Sometimes confrontations may be necessary. Yet other times today's workplace dynamics may escalate misunderstandings into major rifts. For instance, we all know emails are best at communicating information but not nuance. Email wars easily erupt. One supervisor in a small company critiqued a message from a direct report, who fired back that he was being unfair. He fired back that he was just telling her the facts for her own good, and she whipped back a heated response. The war quickly became common knowledge and it took several face-to-face meetings between them to calm the waters and get both of them back on track.

WHEN CULTURES CLASH, workplace conflicts escalate. Globalization means disparate entities often have to mesh: corporations and government, colleges and suppliers, one nation's manufacturing and another's marketing. For instance, Swedish companies acquiring American businesses and Americans taking over Swedish companies have run into sharp edges from differences in cultural work patterns. The two countries may seem similar, but Sweden's heavy emphasis on leadership through teams and America's emphasis on individual leadership create plenty of misunderstandings.

Such clashes are common, from grand scales of international commerce to local enterprises. But, as Jackson's story demonstrates, they don't have to "sink" the organization. Jackson, fresh out of college, signed on to work on a whale-watching boat in Maine and found himself in the middle of tensions between the salty sea captain and academic researchers. They came from different worlds and had far different concerns and perspectives. The researchers had hired the captain, who didn't value their presence but liked the credibility they brought.

"We were paid only by the trip, as was the captain," said Jackson, "so storms and bad weather meant no income. At times the captain was gruff and took out his frustrations on us. We never knew what mood he might be in, and when he was in a bad one, some of the researchers onboard would be feisty right back. But most of them just endured his gruffness. They figured the next day he would be fine, and he usually was. That strategy worked for me. I kept my head low, enjoyed the sightings of the humpback whales, and realized everyone on that boat had their priorities, problems, and oddities."

Exactly! Realizing our differences and "oddities" is a huge step toward defusing conflict.

Most of us are aware of the various tools that help us understand ourselves and others, from Myers-Briggs to the Enneagram to books of psychology and anthropology. What differences there are among us! Sometimes it's hard to celebrate them, sometimes we have to grin and bear it, and sometimes we're forced to make hard choices.

## SURVIVAL STRATEGIES

**CREATE YOUR OWN AGENDA.** Don't let someone who's squelching you or is maddeningly mean determine your responses. Refuse to add to the venom. As Amelia, Ross, and the young professor did, decide what will be best for you in the long run and tie your emotions to your positive plans.

**HELP THE WOUNDED.** If verbal knives are piercing you, others may be bleeding as well. Reaching out to them with a ray of hope or a nugget of counsel may help them and at the same time lift your own spirits.

**POUR OIL ON CHOPPY WATERS.** Attitude pollution is contagious, but so is a positive spirit. Are sarcasm and character assassination common? Counter with gratitude and appreciation in whatever ways you can. Hopefully you can find others of like mind and spirit who can help defuse those deadly explosives.

**REV YOUR ENGINES.** Consider Henry Ford's advice: "When everything seems to be going against you, remember that the airplane takes off against the wind, not with it."

## LEADERSHIP LESSONS

HUMILIATIONS and debilitating demands make some cringe at advice to thrive on change. The words can grate on nerves like fingernails on a blackboard. "Yeah, right! You try all that in this soul-sickening place."

Yet there's a remarkable legacy to the practice of choosing one's attitude despite extreme circumstances. Austrian psychiatrist Victor Frankl, imprisoned in a Nazi death camp, concluded despite the horrors and gross humiliations, "Forces beyond your control can take away everything you possess except one thing, your freedom to choose how you will respond." He viewed men of courage in the concentration camps "comforting others and giving away their last piece of bread" as proof that in any circumstance, we can choose our own attitudes.

Whereas gratitude is the healthiest emotion of all, bitterness and rage tear us apart. It turns out the admonition to have "an attitude of gratitude" is far more than warm motherly advice. Stacks of recent books and articles tell us people feeling gratefulness in their daily lives are more likely to get along with others, sleep better, be less depressed, and have better overall physical health. They also achieve more, have more friends, and avoid burnout.

## QUESTIONS FOR DISCUSSION

- *What is more hurtful to you—a negative comment or an indirect message sent by sarcasm?*

- *When a colleague says something offensive or mean, how do you manage yourself and not add to the negative environment?*

- *Under what conditions do you think it's best not to confront a colleague and "fight for your rights"?*

"Resisting change in the twenty-first century is as futile as wishing there were no taxes."

Paul White

"When you're through changing, you're through."

Bruce Barton

"Don't find fault. Find a remedy."

Henry Ford

## CHAPTER SIX

# RABBITS ON THE FREEWAY

### FINDING HEALTH AND CAPACITY AMID ALL THE NOISE AND FUMES

HIGH STRESS in many organizations is a given. For instance, a manager in a communications company told us, "When I read in a magazine about what happened to some rabbits on the freeway, I just stared at the wall. I thought, That's just what's happening to me!"

The manager had chanced on an article about researchers wondering what would happen if they set up pairs of rabbits to live on the grass between the lanes of an LA freeway. The rabbits would be relatively safe with fences, but they would be exposed to the constant sounds and fumes of passing cars and trucks. It turned out the experiment was a disaster for the rabbits. Living on the freeway did all sorts of things to their brains and nervous systems. They failed to thrive, and their baby bunnies died.

The study drove home the obvious: it's hard to thrive in modern fumes and noise.

"Most days I feel just like those rabbits," the manager said. "I'm never off duty, and the pressure to get it all done never stops."

We've found many workers at all levels feel a lot like those rabbits on the freeway.

At a seminar coauthor Paul White conducted, several customer service representatives for an insurance agency described what happens to them when big storms hit businesses they insure. The minute their offices open, clients desperate for immediate help are calling. Their damaged businesses are on hold and they can't afford to wait for the money to get them moving again. The reps feel overwhelmed by the urgency and volume of the demands.

In most fields, customer service reps deal daily with upset customers, messed-up orders, and constant pressures to stay calm and professional. Stress is ubiquitous. The pressures to "do more with less" and to "run a tight ship" may increase productivity, but often at significant cost to those on the front lines. In downsized organizations, workers endure the stress of picking up others' work and fearing for their own jobs.

A technical writer named Philip worked for eight years during wave after wave of layoffs, anxiously wondering if he would be among those let go. Employees identified as being terminated would receive a message at 6 a.m. to come to a conference-room meeting. Philip told us, "Knowing that might be in my inbox any morning felt to me like waiting for a knock from the secret police. It could come any time."

"I could lose my job tomorrow! Without it, I can't make ends meet. To say the least, I feel stressed out a lot of the time."

Many employees live with that anxiety.

Philip eventually got that notice in the inbox, went to one of those meetings, and was laid off. Fortunately he was given five months to find a new job and gained new employment—but in a different field requiring new skills. He feels relatively safe from layoffs now but is quick to say he's learned there's no real security in today's workplace.

How did Philip handle those eight years of worrying the "secret police knock" might come at any time? "What helped me the most was reading *Executive Blues* by G. J. Meyer. I saw how others go through really crazy stuff and recognized I just have to handle the craziness and take it day by day."

Just handle the craziness? Just handle the stress and near-impossible demands? Easier said than done! Yet whether work cultures are toxic or wonderful, handling stress and anxiety almost always comes with the territory.

A manager named Jared led a small team in a local newspaper business in the South and in 2009 was suddenly confronted with dramatic changes that brought on plenty of stress and anxiety. Here's what he told us:

> When the economy tanked, I found myself no longer doing the job I had loved for nearly 25 years. I'd set the vision for my department and led with confidence and passion. We'd won numerous awards for our hard and creative work, but all that changed. I wasn't let go, but it was very painful to watch people I cared deeply about forced to leave.
>
> My responsibilities shifted drastically, and I've been moved from office to office, leaving me feeling like an office nomad. I manage a couple of employees, but they're younger and more tech-savvy than I, and I'm not always sure how to lead them. I'm a fish out of water—or a manager way out of his element.
>
> On top of that are all the financial pressures because I'm looked to for "breakthrough ideas" to help get the company back into the black. I could

lose my job tomorrow! Without it, I can't make ends meet. To say the least, I feel stressed out a lot of the time.

How is Jared surviving day by day? In addition to the support he feels at his church, he has been rereading Thoreau's *Walden* and before work each day studies books of prayer in a coffee shop. He is also intentional about positive self-talk. He tells himself he comes from sturdy stock and knows how to work hard and take what comes. He remembers his father who survived far more difficult jobs.

Jared as a boy once went into the factory where his father worked. Walking under a bare lightbulb, he stared at the burnishing wheels. That's how his father lost an eye from a piece of flying metal from a spinning brush. His father's work damaged his health, but he survived and later in life found a job where he was treated well.

Jared keeps telling himself he'll take what comes and give all his challenges his very best shot.

BUSINESSMAN FRED SMITH OF DALLAS spoke and wrote a great deal about leadership and the workplace, and one of his themes was handling stress effectively. He was fond of quoting Hans Selye, an early stress researcher who wrote *The Stress of Life* and emphasized—as do many today—that stress can debilitate but also generate energy and productivity. Stress is part of life, and we are made to rise to it in rhythms of effort and recovery.

Empowering emotions provide staying power, but revenge, the unhealthiest of all, debilitates. Fred urged in handling anger and desires for revenge, "Put a leash on it! Don't let the rancor of yesterday fester overnight." He worked at not letting that happen to him. On awakening he had a mantra of four positive mental exercises to start his day, and those included gratitude.

After a remarkable lifetime in business, Fred kept advising and mentoring, even when in his eighties his kidneys failed. Though bedridden, on Saturdays a couple dozen leaders from Dallas would gather around his bed seeking his insights and counsel. They called it "Fred in the Bed." Instead of dreading his thrice-weekly dialysis, he would invite someone to meet him at the hospital for a lively talk during the procedure. He called it "Dialysis University."

Fred passed away, but you can visit still-active breakfastwithfred.com and find plenty of lively counsel. For instance, when you feel like a rabbit on the freeway you might want to consider how he dealt with stress and anxiety. He advised living in "day-tight compartments," a nice mental image to capture advice that's been around a long time. After all, Jesus said, "Don't be anxious about anything; today's troubles are enough to handle."

Michael Lee Stallard, president of E Pluribus Partners, found significant stress relief through "the protective power of connection," particularly when his wife Katie was diagnosed with advanced ovarian cancer. His daughters were twelve and ten years old and the thought of their losing their wonderful mother made him anxious and stressed. Yet family and friends regularly brought food, encouragement, and joy into their home. "Feeling connected to our family, friends, and the Lord lifted our spirits," Michael says. "Although the stress I felt could have immobilized me, our connections protected me. This year we celebrated Katie's tenth year in remission."

Michael is the primary author of *Fired Up or Burned Out: How to Reignite Your Team's Passion, Creativity, and Productivity.* "Today," he says, "I train leaders how to connect and create cultures of connection. I advise them not to worry alone. I teach them to intentionally connect with others by getting to know people's stories and their languages of appreciation in the workplace, asking co-workers questions unrelated to work and finding interests in common—and remembering the simple gestures such as making eye contact and using first names. Just connect, I tell them, and you will experience greater productivity, wellness, and joy in life."

SOMETIMES MADDENING COLLEAGUES generate more stress than time crunches or work volume. A manager named Bethany felt constant stress from a senior team member who dumped her own work on her, resulting in sixty-hour weeks with no overtime pay and too little time with her young family. What was so infuriating was how unnecessary it all was: the older woman would change processes, fail to communicate key details, and drum up unneeded tasks so Bethany would end up working ten-hour days to get four hours of real work done.

Here's how she describes her work group:

> It's hostile because the "senior manager" wants it her way or the highway. She keeps her thumb on everything so she can take all the credit. I go above and beyond, but she keeps telling me I'm not doing my job and broadcasts that to others. She's quick to point out minor mistakes and unnecessarily redoes my work—and complains she has to do it! She's constantly critical. Our department took the Five Languages of Appreciation course, but she considered it pointless.
>
> Outside our workgroup, she's not this way. She jokes with people on the phone, goes out to have a beer, and is always pleasant. With us she's short,

has unattainable expectations, and micromanages to an extreme. She's a workaholic—here sixty hours a week and is also an assistant manager at a store.

I was a manager at my previous employment and never treated my coworkers as if they were beneath me. I have never been treated this unfairly and disrespectfully and have considered changing departments or quitting altogether.

Bethany surely needs to do something. Whatever her course of action, she'll likely continue to feel the stress. And don't we all these days!

Coauthor Gary Chapman recalls the experience of a friend named Nate who for fifteen years at a manufacturing company felt little stress, enjoying his work and liking the people he worked with. But then the economy took a dive and the company downsized. Nate hated to see some of his fellow workers dismissed, but he understood. Production was down and he was just glad to have a job.

"I felt totally unappreciated for all the years I had given the company. So I quit with no place to go."

However, within eighteen months the company got a huge contract with the government. The workload increased, but they did not hire new employees, so that meant more work for those who survived the layoffs. Here's what Nate told Gary:

It became unbearable. I dreaded going to work each day. The stress level was high, employees complained, but management wouldn't listen. They told us we were not reaching our potential. I don't know what they thought I was capable of doing, but I knew

> I couldn't do any more. I threatened to quit and was told by my supervisor, "That's your choice."
>
> I couldn't believe he was so callous. He had no heart. I felt totally unappreciated for all the years I had given the company. So, I quit with no place to go. My wife was upset, but I just could not take it anymore. If they had expressed some concern, I would have been willing to try to work something out, but when I saw I was unappreciated, that was the last straw for me.

Within three months Nate got another job. He tells Gary he is now completely happy in his new environment.

## SURVIVAL STRATEGIES

**UNDERSTAND THE NATURE OF STRESS.** We experience stress when demands are greater than the resources needed to meet it. But our own perceptions can increase our stress. We have to learn to manage our expectations.

**BUILD EMPOWERING HABITS.** A man in his mid-seventies who had created a multibillion-dollar conglomerate surprised us by his candor about his personal routines. "It's all about building the right habits," he told us, "and I'm still working at them right now." Establishing positive habits takes determination throughout life, yet it's worth it—habits can free and empower. Each one contributes to our capacity to handle the pressures and pains of both work and life.

**RECOGNIZE THAT HABITS TRUMP WILLPOWER.** Recent research points out we all have very limited willpower!

That's where habits come in—we need them to kick in when willpower is weak. The remarkable power of good physical, mental, and spiritual habits is well documented. At times we may get discouraged at our failures to keep resolutions. Yet like the successful executive in his seventies, we can find habits empowering us the way our bodies often do on "autopilot."

**DO SOMETHING PHYSICAL.** For those of us who roll our eyes at exhortations to get buff, the latest research makes abundantly clear that adding even a little exercise to a sedentary life makes a huge difference. As one executive said, "Exercise is the easiest part of the puzzle. For me, it's delivered the biggest payoff."

## LEADERSHIP LESSONS

PASSENGERS STREAMED through the Dallas airport late one afternoon as coauthor Harold Myra wearily entered a book stall and scanned the shelves. As CEO of his publishing organization he'd been rushing from meeting to meeting with trustees and business contacts, studying his budget for a new product launch and considering solutions to a sudden personnel crisis. The stress and weight were grinding him down.

A title on a shelf arrested his attention: *The Corporate Athlete.*

It intrigued him. What did that odd word combination mean? He bought the book, and on the flight back to Chicago, he devoured it.

What inspired Harold was how author Jack Groppel paired realism about "the crucible of corporate high performance" with practical ways to mentally change body chemistry, reenergize throughout the day, and deal with the powers of emotions.

Groppel developed his book through the executive training center he cofounded that applies the principles of athletic training to the workplace.

Athletes use stress (physical, mental, and emotional) to become stronger, faster, and more focused. Groppel points out they train for events, but workers have to perform *all* the time and seldom train. He cites the need to adapt a "training mentality" that includes emotional skills, mental preparation, balance, attitude, recovery, fitness, and nutrition as "fundamentals in the training process." He maintains "the human system will do whatever you train it to do."

Harold went on to read books by Groppel's partner, James Loehr, who for years trained top athletes and then began applying what he'd learned with corporate executives. In *Stress for Success* Loehr asserts we have to accept high pressure in the workplace as a fact of life, and to survive and thrive we need to deepen our capacity to handle it. Among Harold's underlines in that book are these:

- As you can increase physical strength by lifting progressively heavier weights, you can systematically train your mind and emotions.
- Emotions run the show in your personal life, in your corporate life, and in your spiritual life. Toughness of the mind and toughness of the body are part of the same continuum.
- Mental training alters brain structure. Empowering thoughts and images stimulate new pathways and, constantly repeated, become stronger.
- Stress is biochemical. The hand that's dealt to you daily at the office, and the number and kind of stressors that flow in and out of your corporate life, are not the determinants

> of your stress level. Your body's internal response dictates everything. The good news is the stress response is highly modifiable. The storms of life and work can be converted into opportunities for expanding stress capacity.

If that last sentence sounds way too facile, perhaps we should revisit our earlier insights from Holocaust survivor Victor Frankl who emphasized our freedom to choose our responses. The pressures and toxins we endure can do deadly damage to our minds and bodies, yet we have quite a bit of control over how we will respond. As Fred Smith advised, choose an attitude of gratitude and "live in day-tight compartments." And as Loehr counsels, "When you are pushed to your absolute limits, affirm to yourself, 'I can deal with this. I can make this day work for me.'"

## QUESTIONS FOR DISCUSSION

- *What in your life (work or personal) is creating the most stress for you currently?*
- *What aspects of the stress (greater demands or fewer resources) are under your influence?*
- *What attitude or perceptual adjustments could you make to help you endure the stress better?*
- *What physical activity or additional sleep could you add to your life to help you manage the stress better?*

"We fail to reckon with the reality of human nature. None of us is totally altruistic."

Gary Chapman

"How frail is humanity! How short is life, how full of trouble!"

the Book of Job

"Every manager at every level has an opportunity, big or small, to do something. Don't pass the buck."

Bob Anderson

# CHAPTER SEVEN

# DESCENT TO THE DARK SIDE

## GREAT PLACES CAN GO DOWN ALARMINGLY FAST

AS WE'VE COLLECTED workplace stories, we've been disconcerted by how often fine organizations lose their momentum—and much worse. Over and over we hear descriptions of "the way it was in the good times" contrasted with steep descents. Sometimes it's because a board selects a leader ill-equipped for the role. Other times, crises cause a rash of bad decisions, or external events crush an organization's spirit and resilience, or internal squabbles spread and infect everyone.

A team leader named Rebecca surprised us by saying she hated her workplace, even though previously she had been enthusiastic about it. "Not anymore," she exclaimed. "Things were really good, but now this place is full of conflict and criticism."

We asked her why and she said it started with management's shift from providing quality services to making money. "Everything's about increasing revenue and decreasing expenditures, with no funds for training or staff development."

She went on: "We never—and I mean NEVER—hear anything positive. But we hear plenty of criticism! They critique us in front of others, like they want to shame us. Employees now come in late and leave early. People are critical of each other and blame each other. I'd leave in a heartbeat if I could."

We all know that a company must make money, but when it becomes the primary focus it wreaks havoc and can cause the best employees to flee. Often we see this in corporate takeovers. Mark, an engineering student in his senior year, told us that's why he quit his job to go back to school. Before a corporate takeover the company's loyal employees never missed a day and loved working together. Mark described his bosses as supportive and he summed up his experience by saying, "We had a wonderful sense of community."

When his company was bought out, everything changed. "The big company said they honored employees," he said, "but they didn't care one bit about us so long as they could make money."

As we interviewed leaders and employees, we found examples like that depressingly numerous and disheartening—and it wasn't always about money. Sometimes just one person at the top would single-handedly ruin a wonderfully effective organization.

Perhaps the most sobering, and for us distressing, example was an organization strongly committed to the values we're emphasizing. Just one leader turned it all on its head. Henry, who spent eight years as a psychologist there, described for us the depth of the organization's earlier determination to honor those high values and then told us what went wrong:

> If you were to review the company staff manual, you would find about 300 pages of progressive communication philosophies—of speaking truth and

> developing a community focused on empathetic, heart-centered counseling. For hundreds of people, the organization made possible life-changing growth dealing with emotional obstructions. It was common for staff to cite working there as the single most important thing they had ever done, with gratitude for an endless stream of insights, self-development, and acquired wisdom.
>
> However, in my eight years there I saw a turn toward the definitive dark side.
>
> Deep within our director's mind and heart, empathy began to fade. It was replaced by an almost mechanical, corporate-esque, take-no-prisoners, problem-solving philosophy. The director designed a process to correct anyone who obstructed this—or, God forbid, was guilty of human error. The forceful use of "conversational 2x4s" was used to verbally "slap persons on the head and wake them up" so they would meet performance expectations.
>
> Ironically, the director's use of "intentional speech and non-violent communication" was impeccable as he made shaming accusations "out of integrity" to address "failure to meet agreements." People would come out of meetings with him emotionally distraught and unable to work effectively for days.

As we listened to Henry's story, we wondered how, in an organization with such elaborately crafted value statements and commitments, the clever use of the values themselves could be used to so completely subvert them. Henry told us he and his colleagues eventually agreed that hidden anger and intolerance brewed deeply in the director—yet in debate he used his experience, knowledge, and intelligence to erect an unassailable fortress.

Here is Henry's further description of the organization's descent:

> The director's dysfunctions grew like a dark cloud over the entire community. Policies changed. Everything became tighter, less trusting, more suspicious. Hidden cameras were installed to monitor staff behavior. The director blamed people for "failures" and dismissed their protests with high-communications shaming terms like "faux feelings." He crafted a life of holding up mirrors for others for so long that he forgot how to look in one.
>
> Employees were driven to do more, more, and more, and no one could measure up to the perfection demanded in the name of progress, growth, and organizational achievement. Eventually it all collapsed. In a single season, 85 percent of the staff left.
>
> I departed with a sour taste in my mouth. I keep in touch with the very few who stayed, and the director is still there. The warm, illumining light once in that place is almost entirely gone.

PAINFUL REALITIES surface in the wake of this story, and it raises the question of why boards often fail to fire malignant bosses. Henry's director brilliantly subverted the organization's core values, yet qualified staffers were squelched in their attempts to call him on it. Unfortunately, a smart high achiever at the top can be nearly impervious to counsel by those affected by the dysfunction. That's why, as the ultimate authorities, trustees on governing boards must know enough about what's really happening to be alerted, to review the organization's health, and to take corrective action when it's needed.

Too often, no alert is sounded. Thoughtful observers ranging from management expert Peter Drucker to the *Harvard Business Review* have made scathing assessments of typical board ineffectiveness. Those who serve as trustees too often see it as an honor or as a perk, failing to help ensure key board functions are implemented. Trustees may think an organization that's meeting its budget and goals is functioning well, yet it may be deviating from its most important values.

As mentioned in chapter 2, Max DePree cautions that work cultures are fragile in many ways.

Henry, now effectively leading a different organization, says deviance can start when leaders' outward adherence to positive models outweighs their spirit. "Empathy that merely follows words isn't authentic," he told us. "People instantly sense it." This has been our experience in training organizations using *The 5 Languages of Appreciation in the Workplace*. There is a profound difference between "going-through-the-motions" employee recognition and authentic appreciation.

Sometimes leaders' successes in one field lead to blunders in another. A gymnastics instructor named Matthew watched that happen, powerless to do anything when new ownership took over his gym.

Matthew was working on the West Coast in the largest and most prestigious gymnastics facility in the state. The new husband-and-wife owners were in their late fifties, wealthy, intelligent—and arrogant. They projected that they had the formula for life and, with deep pockets, assumed they could own a gym and take it to the next level. They hired an experienced general manager who purchased new equipment, had walls freshly painted, and hired more people. Student enrollments surged, money flowed, and it seemed things were going well.

Yet from the beginning, the new owners showed no respect for the managers and instructors. Although they were all seasoned professionals doing their best, they were viewed as "problem employees." After about six months the owners decided the gym was not generating enough profit and suddenly demanded deep cuts in expenses. Matthew was told his salary would be cut by a third, a powerful statement of how he was valued. He felt forced to quit, and one by one the other professionals did the same.

In less than a year after it was purchased, the iconic gym was shut down. Students and parents were shocked and outraged, but they could do nothing. The coaches and staff were all out of work, and the gym was converted into a brewery.

Matthew says that previous to the gym's demise, he had been naïve about how much attitudes at the top of the power pyramid affect everyone below it. "It was the first time I saw a business just disappear," he says. "It happens: I think of Blockbuster, Circuit City, and lots of others. I've learned to be tough-minded about what could happen and to hopefully be at least mentally prepared for dramatic changes."

Some failures, of course, come because of overwhelming market forces or other external shifts. But others like the gym fail because leaders don't lead.

You may recall in chapter 3 a sales manager named Kevin whose boss inspired him and for many years made his company thrive. It was a fine company, with great chemistry and success, and John, his boss, had led with sensitivity and vision. Yet when John moved up to become chairman of the board, he made one very large mistake.

Here's Kevin's short version of what happened when the board was deciding on a new CEO:

> The choice was between a man named Frank and me. John (the current CEO) and the board chose Frank.
>
> Although I didn't necessarily think I was perfect for the job, I knew that Frank definitely wasn't. I believed his personality and management style were so contrary to what the company needed that he would run it into the ground.
>
> When John as outgoing CEO came into my office and asked if I was doing okay, I told him exactly what I thought and gave numerous examples of why I thought Frank was a disastrous choice. I strongly considered leaving.
>
> However, after an evening thinking about it, I knew I wouldn't leave my job. The next day I went to both John and Frank and told them I'd stay and do all I could for the company.
>
> With Frank as CEO, things deteriorated drastically. He led by intimidation and wouldn't make decisions for fear of being wrong. Insecure, he would stand on the other side of someone's cubicle and listen to phone conversations or stand out of sight trying to hear hallway conversations. The environment became negative and cynical, and plenty of angry feelings built up in me.

"With Frank as CEO, things deteriorated drastically."

> I eventually left the company because of a personal illness, but I've kept in touch. After years of inept management that caused huge financial losses, Frank was terminated. John later admitted to me that he and the board had made a huge mistake in choosing the wrong person as his successor.

Frank was an insider, and on paper he seemed to have the right qualifications. John and the board obviously thought he could handle the job. Yet they made the wrong choice.

Somehow they were blind to the incredible power of corporate chemistry—both positive and negative.

## SURVIVAL STRATEGIES

**WATCH FOR WARNING SIGNS.** Change keeps accelerating, and even in the best of organizations, new demands, transitions, and failures to meet expectations bring temptations to short-circuit best practices. Whatever your position, if you see something that bothers you, think through your personal best practices in light of what's going on.

**AFFIRM THE STATED VALUES.** Most organizations have written values commitments. Match them against what you see happening.

**PUT YOUR OAR IN.** Maybe you have power to keep the organization on track, maybe not. But as that old phrase about good folks doing nothing indicates, your oar in the water might make just enough difference. And in situations like Matthew's gym, you might as well bail out of there as soon as the steep downhill slide becomes clear.

# LEADERSHIP LESSONS

PETER DRUCKER as a small boy in Austria learned early that good times don't always last. World War I started, and young Peter lost many loved ones and nearly starved to death. Years later he wrote against the Nazis, and they burned what he had written. During that war, Winston Churchill put Drucker's book *The End of Economic Man* into every new officer's kit.

Drucker became widely known as the father of modern management. A deep conviction informed his lifetime of writing books and articles that transformed organizations and profoundly influenced leaders worldwide. That conviction was this: we are all made in the image of God.

This got him in trouble with General Motors when he wrote about their management practices, for Drucker saw employees not as mere assembly-line producers but as persons. For decades he wrote his seminal works with that core value, in his eighties and nineties helping nonprofits while still producing books and major magazine articles. "If a collapse comes," he presciently told a group of nonprofit leaders, "it will be a moral collapse." He warned against excessive executive compensation and the self-centered practices that contributed to the global economic traumas soon after his death.

If we believe we are made in God's image, we then see—as did Drucker—large implications for the workplace. One is how we view and interact with our colleagues and bosses.

This chapter, "Descent to the Dark Side," addresses organizations going from healthy to toxic—yet the truth is, few of us escape dark-side dynamics, even in thriving cultures. A promise is broken, or a theft is discovered, or a partner betrays us. Friends become enemies.

Sages through the centuries have written of what appears nonsensical: the value of enemies. Fred Smith in *You and Your Network* devotes a chapter to this, observing, "Enemies may threaten our security, our well-being, our prosperity, but we see past them to the good that can come—which prompted Robert Browning to write, 'Then welcome each rebuff that turns life's smoothness into rough.'"

Rebuffs may contain truths. Opposition refines and toughens us.

Fred aligns his thoughts with Jesus' challenge to love our enemies, advising tough, disciplined love, forgiving them because it "frees us from the acid of enmity."

Good times don't always last. Great organizations can lose their momentum. Life and work are difficult for all of us. But we can choose our attitude. And we can seek common cause with those of like spirit who see positive potential in persons and in our fragile workplaces.

## QUESTIONS FOR DISCUSSION

- *When negative events occur in your workplace, what emotions and reactions do you struggle with?*
- *If you let unhealthy reactions grow and begin to act on them, what might happen to you?*
- *What positive actions or preventive steps could you take to survive and thrive?*

"It's amazing what you can do when you don't seek all the credit. I find nothing is really one person's idea."

Dan Tully

"But among you it will be different. Whoever wants to be a leader among you must be your servant."

Jesus

"Servant leaders listen and learn from those they lead. They avoid the trap that so many so-called leaders experience—the arrogance of ignorance."

Bill Pollard

CHAPTER EIGHT

# Rx FOR CYNICISM

## RECOGNITION EVENTS CAN BACKFIRE, BUT AUTHENTIC APPRECIATION EMPOWERS

IN A SMALL SPECIALTY hospital, employees had gathered with coauthor Paul White for a training session on communicating appreciation in the workplace. One of the nurses raised her chin, looked directly at Paul, and said exactly what she was feeling: "I haven't heard anything positive about my performance for two years. Now we're going through this training, and you expect me to believe them when they tell me they appreciate me? That's not going to happen!"

Paul had heard such blunt words before in his work with supervisors and working groups. At first all the cynicism and negativity he encountered surprised him, but eventually he concluded it was common in all sorts of organizations. For instance, when he would ask about employee recognition programs, he'd see sighs and a rolling of eyes. He'd hear sarcastic comments like, "Yeah, we have an employee recognition program," followed by, "But it's a joke. No one takes it seriously. You get a certificate, or a special parking space. Whatever."

Many employees resented management initiatives such as a new corporate tagline or a "we-care-about-our-customers" emphasis. Why? One middle manager told Paul, "It's hard to get employees to believe the company cares about customers when the decisions and policies coming down from the top focus on boosting company profitability by reducing customer service!"

Research shows when team members feel valued, customer satisfaction ratings rise. How ironic, then, that "promoting" appreciation within the workplace often does the opposite.

Recently Paul was chatting with a friend, an executive manager for a large private company, who happened to comment, "Yes, I had to go to our annual service award banquet on Thursday." He explained he had to go every five years.

"So, what it's like?" Paul asked. "What happened?"

"Nothing big. Every year it's the same.Those getting awards line up, your name is called, and you walk across the stage.You're given a plaque, you shake the CEO's hand, get your picture taken with him, and then walk off the stage."

Paul asked what he thought about it.

"Really, it's crazy. They do the same kind of program every year. It's meaningless and a waste of time. But you have to go."

A waste of time. That's a common complaint. For instance, a consultant comes into an organization, does some staff training, and employees are supposed to give compliments to coworkers or write thank-you notes. Everyone may be forced to participate, whether or not the compliments are genuine. After a few weeks it's on to the next "flavor-of-the-month" training, perhaps a personality assessment program. People often feel the whole process is a show to make management look good. The employees feel put upon, go through the motions, do what they're told (sometimes sincerely, but more often, superficially), and view the program as a joke. This repetitive process breeds an underlying distrust.

Sometimes the source of cynicism isn't due to management missteps. People bring their own wounds to the workplace. Many feel they have the right to be cynical because others close to them have repeatedly hurt and failed them, and they've lived difficult, painful lives. Cynicism is essentially a distrust of motives—that others are not genuinely interested in anyone but themselves. Those with a cynical point of view often have an angry edge, their cynicism less about the specific situation and more about how they view life. They've concluded people can't be trusted and that trusting others opens you to being taken advantage of or getting hurt.

With deeply wounded workers, managers might probe with questions like, "Why do you feel the program is insincere? What could be done differently to make it work for you?" Perhaps a small ray of light would come and changes could be made.

Yet in light of the many stories in the previous chapters, it's easy to understand how recognition programs can alienate instead of inspire.

HOSPITALS, SCHOOLS, AND AGENCIES of the government with their inevitable bureaucracies are natural greenhouses for cynicism. Companies subject to heavy government regulations experience the same toxic fertility. Rules and regulations trump common sense, and workers hunker down.

A refinery security officer named Caleb was smart enough to recognize ways employees might react to the rigid government rules and regulations set in place after 9/11 to protect the refinery from terrorists. New to the job, his post-college degree had nothing to do with oil, but without other options he had accepted the position. Though inexperienced, he was charged with making sure the refinery was in full compliance with the stringent government mandates.

For someone untrained, that was a daunting assignment, and soon after his starting, a terrorist hostage drill was scheduled that would include the FBI, four police units, two swat teams, negotiators, and, of course, all the employees. Caleb was told as compliance officer he'd be responsible for coordinating it. More immediately, he was to lead monthly security meetings with the employees. Here's what he was thinking as he faced all this:

"As I looked at the operators sitting in front of me I knew they were thinking, 'You talk like you're one of us, but we both know you're not.'"

> At my first meeting I was apprehensive since there were plenty of combustibles such as resentments at hierarchy and blue-collar/white-collar tensions. It was "we" versus "they." Everyone wanted to be prepared in case of a terrorist attack or a hostage situation, but I was viewed as mostly just there to make life more difficult. As I looked at the operators sitting in front of me in their dirty coveralls, fresh from working in dangerous conditions, I knew they were thinking, *You talk like you're one of us, but we both know you're not.*

Caleb knew he was in a dangerous position with the operators if he couldn't back up his talk with action. A primary source of cynicism is when organizations talk about being a great place to work but fail to make that happen. He knew he had to show he understood their problems, but he also knew he had to find practical ways to address them.

> I saw I had to help them realize I wasn't going to just shove government red tape at them. These new rules were a big pain, and I did feel genuine empathy.

I told them I understood how difficult this was for them and that we'd simplify it as much as possible, then went on to express strong appreciation for their demanding work.

As I said these things, I could see their faces soften and relax.

We followed through on our promises and went to bat for them. One regulation required each employee to drive to a designated location for a background check to get a new identity card, but we worked it out so they could get the cards on-site. The wheels of government grind slowly, with plenty of annoyingly squeaky wheels, and it took a year and a half to get those cards—but we streamlined and simplified as much as we could.

My boss was an interesting character, a Vietnam vet. He had worked in the refinery as a rough-and-ready operator, a simple guy with a great sense of humor. Employees respected him, and he had a gift for defusing tensions. I had lots more formal education than my boss and could have made the huge mistake of feeling superior to him. Instead, he became a great mentor and guide. I was very happy to learn from him.

As I look back, the reasons my years there became such a sweet spot in my life started with my genuinely empathizing with the workers and realizing the impact of what I had to require of them. My expressing heartfelt appreciation for them helped them realize I valued them as persons and recognized the importance of their demanding work.

Appreciation broke down the barriers.

WHAT'S THE ONE thing that most affects how much people enjoy their jobs? First and foremost, people thrive when they feel *appreciated* by their supervisors and colleagues—and that means they sense the appreciation is heartfelt and authentic.

Surveys repeatedly find benefits are not the key factor in worker satisfaction. More important are feeling they're genuinely appreciated in the company and that their jobs make them feel they're part of something meaningful.

Companies have gotten that message, and employee recognition programs have proliferated, with estimates as high as 90 percent of US organizations having them. Yet, remarkably, at the same time employee satisfaction has *decreased*. Many managers are frustrated and confused about how to support and encourage their staffs.

It's been said the human spirit needs praise the way flowers need rain and sun. Flowers without moisture and light wilt, and people without affirmation wilt, too. But you can't simply pour appreciation on people like rain falls on flowers. Not everyone feels appreciated in the same way. Appreciation must be expressed in language and actions most important to the recipient.

In the Survival Guide and Toolkit that follows, we address ways to communicate what has proven to be essential—authentic appreciation. We tag it as the "antidote for cynical cultures."

You'll find lots of other practical and easy-to-read tips in the guide. You can dip in and out and hopefully find insights to meet your needs.

AS STUDS TERKEL observed, work is about "violence to the spirit as well as the body." He wasn't referring particularly to toxic bosses or cultures but workers in a broad range of jobs facing demands and realities requiring courage and resilience.

Work is difficult, and sometimes leading in the workplace most difficult of all. No wonder so many books are written about leadership!

A recent volume from the health-care industry is titled *Leadership in the Crucible of Work.* Typically we hear "crucible" applied to extreme pressures, such as "the crucible of war" or "the crucible of the US presidency." After all, a crucible is "a hollow area at the bottom of a furnace" where metals are refined with extreme heat. But Sandy Shugart, long-time leader of a network of hospitals and now a college president, writes in his book that both leaders and people in ordinary jobs experience the heat and pressure of the work crucible. It's unavoidable and when toxic, the heat sears with special pain.

Shugart writes, "I know a leader of a great servant organization in our own community whose organization has been so damaged by the toxicity of his habits of control and manipulation that no one can work there long without sustaining permanent wounds. Outwardly, he projects competence, wisdom, even servanthood, but his staff knows him as a deeply conflicted, punishing leader. His own unhappiness in this miserable condition only adds to the vitriol waiting to be unleashed when anyone fails to comply with his ever-shifting expectations. His organization seems from the outside to be effective enough, until we consider what might have been, what creative possibilities have been crushed, and what gifted colleagues have been exiled. And he is gradually awakening to the prison he himself has fashioned. How sad."

Shugart advises we must realize leadership tools "are inherently dangerous to both the leader and the led"—that we must look for signs of erosion in our own characters. For instance, accountability can slide toward coercion, persuasion can become spin, and negotiation manipulation. An authentic leader faces down temptations to follow along with other leaders either above or beside him who poison working relationships.

The best leadership literature insists on integrity, trust, and character. Some of us may lead from the top and others from the middle of an organization or even the front lines. When accusations, infighting, and threats come our way, our natural reactions may be to lash out or affix blame. Yet that further ignites the dysfunctions.

Enter here the Prayer of St. Francis. It's not only the religious who find this well-known prayer psychologically valid and remarkably practical. Its wisdom can be found on countless walls of schools, hospitals, counseling centers, churches, and businesses. It can create a mindset of peace and power. It's very simple, but very different from today's reigning thought patterns:

> Lord, make me an instrument of thy peace. Where there is hatred, let me sow love; where there is injury, pardon; where there is doubt, faith; where there is despair, hope; where there is sadness, joy; where there is darkness, light.

St. Francis's prayer goes on to emphasize consoling others instead of ourselves and to care less about being understood than to understand . . . and to love and forgive. Besides the spiritual values of the prayer are the practical principles—including the power of getting our minds off our own troubles and gaining inner peace. Quite applicable to the workplace today!

## QUESTIONS FOR DISCUSSION

- *Have you gone through a training session that felt superficial? What could have made it feel more genuine to you?*

- *Do you struggle with being cynical about some area at work? Do you mistrust others' motives? If so, why?*

- *Can you identify someone you know or worked with who relates to others authentically? Can you think of ways you'd like to become more like her or him?*

## BONUS MATERIAL

# SURVIVAL GUIDE AND TOOLKIT

EVEN THOSE OF US who have been around the work world for a while can find ourselves blinded by poisonous people and bullying bosses. The sad fact is, they're ubiquitous. In one survey, 64 percent of respondents were currently working with a toxic person, and 94 percent had worked with someone toxic in their career. In a study of nurses, 91 percent said they'd had experiences in which they felt attacked, devalued, or humiliated. And consider this: among those nurses, more than half didn't believe they were competent to respond to the verbal abuse.

That's the reason for this guide! Few of us, no matter how savvy, feel completely competent to cope with the realities of a toxic work setting. We hope this guide will provide a few insights and strategies to help you survive and thrive in your workplace.

## IS YOUR WORKPLACE TOXIC?
### A QUICK TEN-POINT CHECKLIST

☐ 1 Hidden agendas characterize communication and decision-making; issues are not addressed openly.

☐ 2 Departments seldom work together to reach shared goals.

☐ 3 Leaders have the pattern of saying one thing and doing another.

☐ 4 Everyone feels pressured to make things look good.

☐ 5 The managers view people as there solely to get tasks done, with little interest in getting to know them personally.

☐ 6 Supervisors or managers manipulate team members through embarrassment or anger.

☐ 7 Apathy, cynicism, and a lack of hope mark the overall work environment.

☐ 8 Rules and procedures are largely ignored.

☐ 9 Employees sense little accountability for their actions and decisions.

☐ 10 People are "used" for the organization's benefit and discarded when no longer considered useful.

There is no formal scoring of this checklist, but obviously, the more items checked indicate a more toxic environment. An expanded version of this checklist—which will assess ten subscales, generate an individualized report, and identify resources for the most problematic areas—can be found at appreciationatwork.com/toxicworkplace.

# ANTIDOTE FOR CYNICAL CULTURES: AUTHENTIC APPRECIATION

PEOPLE IN THE WORKPLACE desperately want to feel valued and appreciated, but the stark fact is, most do not—not by their organizations, nor their supervisors, nor their colleagues. And when employees don't feel valued, bad things happen.

- They feel discouraged and taken advantage of, and they show up late or call in sick.
- They dislike their work, they don't follow policies and procedures, and productivity goes down.
- Employee theft increases and customer satisfaction decreases.
- Negative attitudes and irritability generate tensions; employee turnover increases.

In contrast, when team members feel valued, positive results follow. Workers are less grumpy, managers enjoy their work, and all persevere more in problem solving. You sense increased loyalty among staff and customers and less sick time and on-site accidents. The research is clear about the benefits.

Organizations are well aware of all that, and most have started recognition programs. Yet many managers and front-line employees view these attempts with cynicism and apathy because they often come across as inauthentic.

How can that be changed? It takes far more than good intentions, as frustrated supervisors have learned. Coauthors Gary Chapman and Paul White address these issues in their book *The*

*5 Languages of Appreciation in the Workplace*, unpacking crucial principles including:

- Communicate appreciation regularly, not just at the annual review or recognition events.
- Make it personal and individual, not for the whole department. Going-through-the-motions recognition is not the same as authentic appreciation.
- Relate appreciation to a specific action or character quality as opposed to a generic "Good job!" And communicate it with authenticity. Find what you can genuinely affirm, even if it seems small, for a small compliment is far better than a forced one. If you don't value your colleague, faking it will make things worse.
- Show appreciation as part of your daily work activities.
- Encourage peer-to-peer appreciation. The chemistry of an organization depends on more than "top-down" morale building.
- Remember that not everyone feels appreciated in the same ways. For instance, not everyone values verbal compliments ("words are cheap"). It's vital to communicate appreciation in the language and actions valued by the recipient, which varies significantly. People have different languages of appreciation, and these include Words of Affirmation; Acts of Service; Tangible Gifts; Quality Time; and Physical Touch.

Within each of these languages, people value different types of actions. For example, some employees whose primary language is Quality Time like personal time with their supervisors, while others prefer to go out to lunch with colleagues. To help supervisors and managers identify specific ways each team member feels valued and encouraged, we developed the *Motivating by Appreciation Inventory* and the other workplace resources listed below for you to explore and utilize.

For more information check out:

- *The 5 Languages of Appreciation in the Workplace*, by Dr. Gary Chapman and Dr. Paul White
- *Motivating By Appreciation Inventory*. www.mbainventory.com
- *Appreciation at Work* resources www.appreciationatwork.com
- YouTube: *Appreciation at Work*
- Facebook: *5 Languages of Appreciation*
- Twitter: @drpaulwhite.

# TOP TEN TRAITS OF TOXIC LEADERS

SO WHY ARE THERE so many bad bosses? While researching this book, we were surprised at the large number of our professional contacts with grim stories to share, and we were equally surprised how many of them had endured toxic bosses for far too long. How could so many intelligent people not rise up sooner rather than later to confront those who were wrecking their lives?

The answers are complicated, as you've seen.

When any of us first join an organization, we're not exactly expecting to find bad apples in high positions, and noxious leaders are often brilliant at making their nastiness seem "natural."

But we should raise a caution here. Work environments don't need toxic leaders to become unhealthy—that happens in many ways, among them ineffective structures or procedures, poor communications, or simply a large number of dysfunctional employees. Identifying these characteristics shouldn't start a blame game where none is warranted.

That said, reviewing these disturbing facts about toxic leaders may bring you some "aha" moments, and seeing through their disguises might save you or a friend considerable pain. Then there's the benefit we hesitate to mention: since we all have our quirks, if while scanning these characteristics we catch the slightest whiff of them in ourselves, we may need to do some soul-searching.

Obviously, toxic leaders come in many varieties, and the severity of their sicknesses varies. Some of these characteristics overlap because so many rise from one core dynamic: their extreme self-centeredness.

**THEY LOOK GOOD (AT LEAST INITIALLY).** They're often articulate, skilled socially, and persuasive. They may be physically attractive, have an impressive resume, or come from a famous or successful family. They can be smart and highly skilled in the technical arena of a business. They gain leadership positions in various ways. Many are hired on the basis of their initial aura of skill and talent. Others know how to excite people with a vision, or they demonstrate they can motivate others to generate positive results. Some slide into power in family-owned businesses or by working their connections. Sometimes they start out as largely healthy individuals but, over time, pressures and compromises degrade their integrity.

**THEY'RE EXTREME ABOUT ACHIEVING GOALS.** Most toxic leaders are intensely committed to achieving goals—or at least, the appearance of doing so. Many have the capacity to cast a vision and motivate, and for those to whom they're accountable, they know how to "give them what they want to hear." Hyper-focused on accomplishment, they use all of their resources to pursue their goal, and they are adept at getting others to complete tasks for them. It is important to note, however, that their goals often are not the same as the organization's goals. Their goals are driven by self-interest and self-promotion, and they will use the organization's resources to help them achieve their personal objectives.

**THEY'RE MANIPULATIVE.** Toxic leaders are masters of manipulation—both of information and people. They're especially adept at image control, making things look good when they're not. They often selectively cite facts to support their positions, manipulating the presentation of information. Some are skilled at manipulating the media to forward their image and to proclaim their success. They choose what they will share, when, with whom, and in what manner, maintaining close control of all of the actual raw data. Through guilt, shame, and threat of embarrassment, toxic leaders manipulate those who work for them, colleagues and strategic partners, and sometimes those for whom they work. They even resort to blackmail, with threats like "If you don't cooperate, you know what's going to happen to you."

**THEY'RE NARCISSISTIC.** Toxic leaders truly believe they're superior—that they're brighter, more cunning, and more talented. They view any good result as due to their talents, efforts, and leadership. As a result of their obvious "superiority," they naturally conclude they should come first: their needs (often lavish), their image, their success. It is all about them, although they often paint the scenario in terms of what is best for the organization or clientele. Although they won't say so publicly, they believe rules don't apply to them but are made for simple people who need them and don't understand their higher cause or calling. When not given the attention they believe they deserve or when they have to share the limelight, they become extremely upset and take it out on those around them. They believe they are the reason for everything good that has happened, and they should get the credit.

**THEY STEAL THE CREDIT FOR OTHERS' SUCCESSES.** Most toxic leaders have no qualms about taking full responsibility for any success or something that looks successful. Whether involved or not, if the positive result occurs near their presence or influence, they'll proclaim the results are due to their superior vision, insight, and efforts. When a team commits to extraordinary time and effort to make an event successful, their work is not mentioned—the leader gets the full glory. It's especially irksome when someone through extremely hard work and long hours turns an impending failure into success. Everyone involved knows who is really responsible, yet the toxic leader takes all the credit and often has the audacity (and capability) to make the true hero look bad in the process.

**THEY'RE CONDESCENDING.** With their narcissistic view of themselves, toxic leaders almost always relate to others in a condescending manner—except when they praise others to manipulate them. They expect to be served by others, regardless of the person's position. Smooth and socially suave in public, they reserve their condescension for the workplace. In public encounters they may act civil and cooperative, but afterward they'll privately ooze their anger and disdain for others.

Since they believe no one else is as talented or bright as they, they think their ideas should always be received with respect and deference. Be forewarned: Do not challenge them in front of others. When they don't feel appropriately respected, they tear down those they see as a threat to their authority. In a meeting they can turn on team members, using insults or rage or sarcasm.

**THEY'RE INAUTHENTIC.** At first, toxic leaders may act as if they care deeply about the organization's cause and its people. In fact, one type of toxic leader is the warm, socially engaging leader who comes across as greatly caring for others. But it's a superficial act to achieve a goal. Over time, their true persona becomes apparent to those around them.

When this façade of caring begins to crumble, some team members respond by working to keep the leader's deficits from being discovered. Why? The team may want to achieve their goals and not look as if they've been duped. Or they may be in a position that will make them look bad if the leader's dysfunctions and actions are found out. So they continue the charade. Others lose trust in the leader, begin to distance themselves, and give in to cynicism.

The leader's lack of authenticity can become evident in other areas as well—they don't have the talents and skills they appeared to have, their prior experience and education may turn out to be a sham, and often the results they bragged about achieving in other organizations are exposed at untrue.

**THEY USE OTHERS.** For the sake of "the larger cause," toxic leaders will use and sacrifice those who work for them, no matter how loyal. When goals are not met or unethical behaviors are about to be exposed, they can become vindictive and sometimes explosive. Most frightening is their quiet anger and veiled threats.

Toxic leaders rarely, if ever, take responsibility for anything that goes wrong. They successfully attribute failure to others. They're talented at rewriting history and coating themselves in Teflon, allowing nothing bad to stick. They'll ask team members, "How could you let this happen? I'm terribly disappointed in you." People can walk out of a meeting asking, "What just happened? How did the boss dodge that bullet?"

**THEY WON'T ADDRESS REAL RISKS.** Toxic leaders tend to ignore issues they don't care about or those that don't help them look good. Issues crucial to the health of the organization, such as conflicts among staff, go unaddressed. In effect, they say to the team, "Duke it out and let me know who wins." Often they focus on immediate gains, neglecting long-term implications or simply saying, "It will all work out over time." Many toxic leaders pay extreme attention to presenting an image of helping the organization succeed financially but ignore the realities of the true financial situation.

**BEFORE THINGS FALL APART, THEY LEAVE.** One thing most toxic leaders know how to do well is when to "get out of town" before everything falls apart and, like the Wizard of Oz, they're discovered behind the curtain. Some "make out like a bandit" financially or leap to a larger organization and into a higher position of leadership and influence—while their former companies clean up the ruin they left in their wake, be it financial disaster, legal problems, a ruined brand, or dysfunctional systems. Unfortunately, some organizations jump from one toxic leader to another because their systems and procedures for hiring are so poor they get snookered again.

## HOW TO DEAL WITH DYSFUNCTIONAL PEOPLE—AND NOT GO CRAZY YOURSELF

IS SOMEONE IN your workplace wrecking its harmony and no matter what anyone says or does, it's just getting more shrill and discordant? We all have to deal with "odd ducks" working with or for us. Whether emotionally unstable, or broken by life, or just plain ornery, their attitudes and eccentricities can go far beyond annoying. Sometimes we may find ourselves feeling the contagion of their negativity or thoroughly bewildered by behaviors that make no sense.

As a psychologist, coauthor Paul White has worked with difficult individuals in a variety of settings. Over time, he came to see common behavior patterns and began describing them as "dysfunctional people." It can be helpful to understand how they think and the rules of life by which they live.

Dysfunctional literally means "problems with functioning." People with dysfunctional patterns have difficulty living within the rules of reality—most notably, with the relationship between choice, responsibility, and consequences. They tend to *deny* they've made a poor choice, preferring to make excuses or blame others. A favorite phrase is "It's not my fault."

Often, even when they are caught in the act of having made a poor choice, they *deflect* responsibility for the action. "Well, *you* should have..." "It's not that big a deal, everyone does it..." "They'll never know..." or "They'll take care of it."

## Key Differences between Functional and Dysfunctional Individuals

| FUNCTIONAL | DYSFUNCTIONAL |
|---|---|
| Honesty, integrity | Deceit, not telling the whole story |
| Direct communication | Indirect communication (talk "through" others) |
| Responsibility comes before privileges | Sense of entitlement |
| Accept responsibility for choices and results | Blame others, make excuses |
| Delay gratification | Have to meet desires now |
| Live in reality on day-to-day basis | Escape from reality (TV, movies, video games, drugs, alcohol, sleep) |
| Save, do without | Spend excessively, go into debt |
| Learn from mistakes | Expect to be rescued from consequences |
| Forgive and let go of past hurts | Hold on to grudges, revenge |
| Keep commitments | Verbal commitments without follow-through |
| Say what they mean | Hidden agendas |
| Being "real" | Focus on image and appearance |
| Can disagree without getting personal | Disagreement leads to anger, personal attacks, and hatred |
| Maintain appropriate personal boundaries | Smother others; use guilt to manipulate |

Finally, dysfunctional individuals *disconnect* their actions from the results that flow from their choices. Sometimes they seem to have a glitch in their brain that they can't see the connection between what they did and the result.

To gain a more complete picture of the behaviors and communication patterns of dysfunctional individuals, please review the chart on the previous page.

Like most personality types, dysfunctional individuals can be found in virtually every level of an organization. However, the more dysfunctional a person is, usually the harder it is for them to advance, especially in healthy organizations where employees and leaders are held accountable.

If you work with people, you will interact with dysfunctional individuals—either as customers, vendors, direct reports, colleagues, or supervisors.

## SIX WAYS TO STAY SANE

LET'S SAY YOU'RE a mid-level manager and examples we give remind you of a toxic behavior that's similar to that of a colleague. Or perhaps one of your direct reports often disrupts work—or maybe you even wonder if a coworker is actually crazy. How do you handle the unpredictable and inappropriate actions of coworkers?

It would take volumes to adequately address that, but here are six boiled-down bits of counsel:

**DON'T EXPECT THEM TO RESPOND "NORMALLY."** No matter what you do, you may find yourself blamed or second-guessed or told you did the worst possible thing when you actually did something good. They may get angry if you talk to them and offended if you don't. To survive such attitudes or the wide variety of other dysfunctions, the sane approach is to give up expectations of getting healthy responses.

**ACCEPT THE FACT YOU CAN'T CHANGE THEM.** You're trying to get through to someone and you think, *It makes so much sense! Why don't you get it!* Working with someone dysfunctional can make you feel like screaming at their stubbornness or what appears to be downright stupidity. Yet the truth is, no matter what you say or do, it's unlikely the person will listen or change. You've got the experience and wisdom, and your life is in a lot better shape, but this person just blows you off. After doing what's kind and forthright, don't lose sleep over it.

Does all this sound hopeless? Can't people change? Yes, they can. But they have to decide they want to change. And often, individuals with severely unhealthy patterns have to hit the wall of reality—that their beliefs about life and their way of living don't work because they don't match the way the world works. In addition, many struggle with mental health issues that distort their perception of reality and block efforts to bring about change.

**SET CLEAR BOUNDARIES.** Be definite about what you will and will not do. You may hear, "You need to fix this because you helped make it go wrong," or that if you were a good person "you would help me out just this once," even though you see a pattern of bad choices. Most of us try to change the other person or give in to their demands, yet giving in reinforces their dysfunctional patterns. Carefully think through your boundaries and then clearly communicate them.

**DON'T ACCEPT FALSE GUILT.** You may be blamed for someone else's problems or made to feel blame for not doing enough—even though all you could do was damage control. Many a dysfunctional person is good at loading guilt on others; ease it off your shoulders.

**DON'T TAKE IT PERSONALLY.** In toxic situations, gaining emotional distance isn't always easy. Yet as a soldier isn't surprised when someone shoots at him, a manager shouldn't be surprised when upsetting things happen. Personal attacks and noxious behavior can jar our equilibrium, but try to gain perspective by considering the source.

**GET AFFIRMATION FROM FUNCTIONAL FOLK.** While dealing with a dysfunctional person, you may feel "fogged" and wonder how well you're handling the situation. Perhaps you thought you had things figured out, but now you're not so sure. Are you thinking clearly and responding appropriately? Check in with thoughtful colleagues who can help you think things through.

# HANDY LIST OF SURVIVAL STRATEGIES

FOR EASY REFERENCE, we gathered the chapter-end Survival Strategies, broadened some a bit, and added a few. Perhaps you'll find some relevant to your situation.

## A Toxic Boss

**GAIN PERSPECTIVE.** Skim through our ten characteristics of toxic bosses. If yours has quite a few, you may need to move on as soon as possible. On the other hand, if your boss has frustrating personality traits but you're not feeling paralyzed or humiliated, maybe you can find ways to adjust. Seek out someone wise to give you objective counsel. Listen for new ways of looking at your boss's actions and what action steps you can take.

**KEEP BITTERNESS AT BAY.** Working for a nasty boss can make you not only angry (which may be useful energy if wisely communicated) but bitter in ways that can make you toxic, too. Find ways to nurture your inner reserves and gain perspective. Develop toughness, but resist embittered resentments. Don't let bad leadership start to sour yours.

**FACE YOUR FEARS.** We all have them, and too often they lurk deep within, sapping our will and clouding our thoughts. Surface them, confront them, and ramp up courage by seeking resources that challenge and inspire you.

**STAND TALL.** Clayton in our first chapter was too inexperienced to know that letting his toxic boss humiliate him would give him a green light to do it again. In the second chapter, Anna firmly confronted her boss when she saw she might become the next victim. Reject the culture of fear. Establish clear boundaries.

**DIVERT THE DEADLY STREAM.** Consider another tip from Anna, who was in a position to lessen the poisonous stream flowing toward others. She was determined to do what she could. Maybe you, too, could keep some of the poison from reaching others.

## You Long to Quit!

**SEE THROUGH THE FOG.** Many of the workers' stories in this book illustrate the importance of figuring out what's happening to you as early as possible. By the time you're longing to quit you may have spent far too much of your life in a toxic situation. Seek clarity about what's really going on and consult with your bases of support and insight.

**ASK YOURSELF THE TOUGH QUESTION.** Are you giving up and pulling the plug too soon? Lots of people in the work force have difficult bosses and work with unpleasant people. Study all the principles for dealing with bad bosses and awful jobs that you can find online and in your library.

**ASSESS YOUR OPTIONS.** Okay, you really want out. In most cases, quitting creates all sorts of fallout, and sometimes it takes time to make the transition. Do a careful assessment of all your possibilities, even if they seem to be few. Network for insights and options.

**LISTEN TO YOUR BODY.** Ruth and Bill in the first chapter finally decided their paychecks weren't as important as their health and sanity, so they quit—but not before serious damage had been done to their mental and physical health. When your body insistently complains, it's time to get that action plan in high gear.

**FACE JOBLESSNESS HEAD ON.** Michael Gill in his Starbucks book mentioned in chapter 3 insists the trauma of losing his job, devastating at the time, was ultimately the best thing that ever happened to him. Joblessness can be rough or even catastrophic for everyone impacted by it, yet it happens. Whether you're in a workplace that's empowering or exploitive, summon courage and a readiness to view whatever happens as the next set of challenges and the next adventure.

## Your Workplace Is a War Zone

**RECOGNIZE EMOTIONS RULE.** Psychologists point out we're more emotional than rational. Although we may think we function by logic and common sense, more often we act and react from our feelings. When emotions roil the waters, take deep breaths and let gratitude for good things and your common sense take over and calm you.

**RESIST RETALIATIONS.** Florence Nightingale advised a long time ago, "Do not engage in any paper wars." Today, beware of email wars—they can escalate your troubles. As indicated in a Chinese proverb, the path of revenge means you dig two graves, and one is yours.

**CREATE YOUR OWN AGENDA.** Don't let others determine your responses. If coworkers are creating a "staff infection" with gossip or internecine warfare or they're demeaning you and spreading poisons, spit out the venom before it can invade your body. Develop positive ways to respond.

**"SCORE OFF" ATTACKS.** Oswald Chambers stated what he called an open fact: "Life without war is impossible." He described health as "requiring sufficient vitality on the inside against things on the outside." Just as our bodies fight off germs, throughout life we deal with all sorts of "deadlies." Chambers said we must nurture spiritual strength to "score off the things that come against us"—an interesting way to think of our responding with vitality to attacks or reversals.

**HELP THE WOUNDED.** If verbal knives are piercing you, others may be bleeding as well. Reaching out to them with a ray of hope or a nugget of counsel may help them and at the same time lift your own spirits.

**POUR OIL ON CHOPPY WATERS.** Attitude pollution is contagious, but so is a positive spirit. Are sarcasm and character assassination common? Counter with gratitude and appreciation in whatever ways you can. Hopefully you can find others of like mind and spirit who can help defuse those deadly explosives.

## Conflict, Overload, and Exhaustion

**UNDERSTAND THE NATURE OF STRESS.** We experience stress when demands are greater than the resources needed to meet it. But our own perceptions can increase our stress. We have to learn to manage our expectations.

**DO SOMETHING PHYSICAL.** For those of us who roll our eyes at exhortations to get buff, the latest research makes abundantly clear that adding even a little exercise to life makes a huge difference. As one executive said, "Exercise is the easiest part of the puzzle. For me, it's delivered the biggest payoff."

**BUILD EMPOWERING HABITS.** A man in his mid-seventies who had created a multibillion-dollar conglomerate surprised us by his candor about his personal routines. "It's all about building the right habits," he told us, "and I'm still working at them right now." A teacher heard us mention that and chimed in, "That's me, too. Years ago I wrote myself a reminder card that said, 'What good habit did you help build TODAY?' I keep working at it—and it's worth it!" Throughout life, habits can free and empower, contributing to our capacity to handle the inevitable pressures and pains.

**RECOGNIZE HABITS TRUMP WILLPOWER.** Recent research points out we all have very limited willpower! That's where habits come in—we need them to kick in when willpower is weak. The remarkable power of good physical, mental, and spiritual habits is well documented. At times we may get discouraged at our failures to keep resolutions, but like the successful executive in his seventies, we'll find habits empower us as our bodies on autopilot do what we in our better moments want them to do.

## New Top Leadership

**WATCH FOR WARNING SIGNS.** Change keeps accelerating, and even in the best of organizations, transitions, new demands, and failures to meet expectations bring temptations to short-circuit best practices. Whatever your position, if you see something that bothers you, think through your personal best practices in light of what's going on.

**AFFIRM STATED VALUES.** Most organizations have written values commitments. Carefully evaluate them and match them against what you see happening. Be supportive and give new leadership the benefit of the doubt, but know what their commitments should be.

**COMPARE BEST PRACTICES.** If you're wondering if what happens in your workplace is simply what "comes with the territory," check out what's happening elsewhere. Network to get a picture of the chemistry and dynamics in similar organizations

**PUT YOUR OAR IN.** Maybe you have power to keep the organization on track, maybe not. But as that old phrase about good folks doing nothing indicates, your oar in the water might make just enough difference.

## Toxic Changes

**SWALLOW HARD AND GET NIMBLE.** Good—even great—workplaces can go bad, as seen in chapter 7. We knew a leader who passed his CEO title on to his son, who proceeded to dismantle much of what his dad had built up. Longtime loyal lieutenants were let go, company stock tanked, and thousands of employees were caught up in the chaos. A "descent to the dark side" can happen swiftly, even in the best of workplaces. Stay alert, prepare yourself mentally and spiritually, and don't let past glories blind you to the realities of what's going on. If you need to bail to survive the storms—don't wait.

**GET TOUGH.** Mental and spiritual toughness go together. Deepen your commitment to your most essential values and mentally rehearse the specific ways you can take positive action. Read a book like *Stress for Success* or *Toughness Training for Life* by James Loehr.

**THRIVE ON CHANGE.** Many of us get tired of hearing that mantra, especially when we must cope with changes disrupting what we most care about. Yet the relentless acceleration of change requires flexibility of all of us, whatever our skills and roles. We are hurtling into the future, and the future will soon be a very different culture. Like an immigrant to a land with different customs and languages, we have to continually adapt and cultivate mindsets that maintain both our integrity and capacity to contribute.

Visit www.appreciationatwork.com/toxicworkplaces for additional resources.

# THE ABUSE OF THE RING OF POWER

## AN INTERVIEW WITH A DOCTOR/ MANAGER/PROFESSOR WHO EXPERIENCED IT

IN OUR RESEARCH for this book we considered Dr. Lauretta Young the perfect person to interview. Who else is a medical doctor with strong management experience who teaches MBAs to lead with integrity . . . and held a top position in a large health care organization . . . and personally experienced the corporate devastation wrought by a toxic CEO?

Dr. Young brings a wealth of insights and professional depth to any discussion of today's workplaces. She has supervised health-care training and quality management and served as chief of a department with over 250 clinicians. She is board-certified in psychiatry and neurology and is currently the Director of Student Resiliency and a professor in the health care MBA program at Oregon Health Services University. What follows is a condensed version of several of our conversations.

*You were mental health chief in a large health organization. Tell us what happened.*

> Delays in billing resulted in 30 percent of revenues lost, and that triggered catastrophic decisions. The board hired a new CEO who, instead of addressing the systemic problems, blamed managers and clinicians. People who had given their lives to the company were let go and crucial organizational memory was lost. The new leader focused on assigning blame. He was ruthless.

*How bad was the damage?*

When I was chief, we had very low turnover. In the four years since I left there's been a 100 percent turnover of psychiatrists, at an astronomical cost to the company. They left because they were being abused.

The provider I'm now with suffered the same stresses—declining revenues, shortage of nurses—yet people here like to come to work, they are treated fairly, and the company is rewarded with creativity and productivity.

What was most toxic was the new leader's trying to find one or two scapegoats to blame instead of solving the problems. I've seen this happen repeatedly. A charismatic narcissist convinces a board of directors he can solve their problems. Then he finds people to blame instead of identifying the systemic problems and equipping and empowering those on the front lines.

*How did you deal with all this personally?*

I realized I wasn't trapped, and I had built pockets of support and security. You don't have to drink the Kool-Aid, and there's always someone to hang out with. But when it became clear I had to leave, it was very sad. I liked the work and the people, but the new leadership thought the people were expendable.

There's so much evidence, so much research based on real-life companies that investing in people means the company does 50 to 60 percent better. This is known. Yet you have mean-spirited people without empathy running some of these organizations. They have serious personality disorders. We call them "divas" running companies.

Unfortunately, there are many stories like this, and boards don't seem to learn.

*How can trustees who have to make these choices get it right?*

They need to separate individual characteristics from systems issues and occasional bad behavior from patterns. Power can corrupt. The thing I love about the Lord of the Rings movies is the truth that some people wear the ring of power better. Clearly there are leaders who are bullies and jerks, and we need strong systems to not allow the abuse of power.

*You've mentioned we are now dealing with serious unintended consequences from the self-esteem movement. How have they contributed to workplace problems?*

When you repeatedly tell children and young adults they are good regardless of what they do—when you give them trophies no matter what—some then become narcissistic and blame others for their own failures. We haven't adequately taught them emotional intelligence, to modulate their anger and inner demons.

*What do you teach your students in your MBA classes? What do you warn them about and what actions can they take?*

Our course is designed to get people to learn to think differently, to avoid the "common thinking" trap.

Individuals get stuck into viewing problems from one viewpoint, which leads to errors in judgments, reactions, and conclusions.

For example, one administrator concluded a doctor had problems with over-hospitalizing because the data showed a significantly higher rate for admitting patients. Yet the doctor frequently worked in the ER on Friday nights and had a different set of patient problems, including violence and drug and alcohol issues. This particular administrator had the reputation of being a bully, verbally attacking people and viewing problems from a blame-the-person viewpoint.

We teach people not to fall into the "common thinking" trap of seeing from just one perspective. We can decrease workplace toxicity by providing more tools, and one is to see problems from different points of view.

We also teach specific actions and skills for relating effectively to others in the workplace. We give them a huge amount of business articles and other research showing how you treat your people results in significantly better financial results.

My favorite author is Jody Gitell, author of *High Performance Healthcare* (2009). For example, if employees communicate in a respectful, accurate manner and within a realistic time frame, they are more likely to get better results in response to their requests and directives. This communication style is directly correlated to profitability and staff retention. We use a number of articles from the *Harvard Business Review* that support this research.

Treating people with respect is not being "soft" but is foundational to business profitability. The chairperson of my department says to my students, "Welcome to the revolution—the revolution to build better business practices and improve financial results."

During our interviews, a remarkable number of well-placed professionals told us tales of highly credentialed health professionals humiliating them.

Many people, regardless of their professional training, treat others poorly. Some of them are ignorant, some are mean, and probably some are evil. We focus on the "ignorant" group to change how they relate to others. We're trying to decrease toxic workplaces by giving people positive skills rooted in solid research-based practices. For example, we use your *5 Languages of Appreciation in the Workplace.*

*If they apply positive principles but find themselves in a workplace with a toxic boss or colleague, how should they respond?*

They should assess how they're being affected. I personally use the test of "energy vampire"—do I feel sucked dry after an interaction with this person? Do I feel victimized?

We teach our students to ask, "What would make a reasonable person act this way?" Behavior is not always based on the individual but includes problems stemming from broader systemic issues.

We also talk a lot about "releasing your adversaries." First, we help the students identify their allies and adversaries. Then we try to help them determine when they need to "release their adversary," which may mean: (a) leaving the organization, (b) reducing the amount of interaction with the person, or (c) releasing them psychologically.

*What other advice about their work do you offer?*

Many people for many reasons feel trapped in toxic work cultures, and they have a lot of hope things will be at least okay. Even after ten or twelve bad things have happened, they still have hope, feeling, "This isn't supposed to be happening." It's amazing how many bad things have to happen before some will leave. They often pay a price for delaying too long.

From my experiences the past ten years I tell my students, "You never know. You may be happy at your work, but don't assume it will go on forever. Develop your network now. Your company could be bought out, money could become the primary value, jobs shipped overseas, and the culture can change immediately. Prepare your ongoing career parachute."

To many, this is a revelation.

# GREEN MEADOWS AND GREAT BOSSES

IN THE DARK, you look for sources of light. Slogging through a toxic swamp, envisioning a green meadow ahead lifts your spirits and widens your perspective.

Before starting this book, we never imagined there were so many toxic bosses. Yet employees also described many good bosses, and even some great ones. That's good to know!

If you ask people if they've ever had a toxic boss, you'd likely be surprised at how many have. But if you ask about *good* bosses, you just may hear plenty of inspiring descriptions.

We liked what Sue Marsh, director of planning at Navitas Wealth Advisors, told us about the confidence she feels knowing a boss has integrity. Here's what she said:

> Two years out of college, I discovered a client had crossed the line from aggressive tax planning into violating tax law. My boss, Bruce, didn't hesitate, waver, or blink; he just calmly stated, "If they aren't willing to fix it, we walk away—we don't go there." Bruce's reaction stuck with me: "We don't go there, period."
>
> Later another boss named Mike took a stand for new employees. We operated in a "figure-it-out-for-yourself" environment; if you learned fast and didn't make mistakes, you got promoted; if not, you left. Mike tired of watching talented young people fail, so he created a guidebook to ease the transition from college to the cubicle.
>
> George, my current boss, always chooses the best solution for a client, even if a perfectly acceptable

> alternative would earn him more money. "This is the better choice," he says. "God's going to honor this decision."
>
> Working alongside a boss with integrity is empowering. Knowing that he will do the right thing, even if it costs him, gives me the freedom to do the right thing too, without fear of repercussions—and allows me to brag about my great boss when others are complaining!

We found refreshing the frequency and depth of appreciation for good bosses. To lift your sights and spirits, here are short profiles by employees of six bosses they love:

## THE MAGNETIC POWER OF HUMILITY

### The Owner/Publisher

FOR DECADES we've been hearing about "greedy CEOs." Yet many successful CEOs have strong faith and care deeply about their employees and their communities. A writer in a communications company told us about his great boss, and here is a short version of all he was eager to share.

> Everyone in our company could tell you how humble our founder is. He's written all these bestselling books and done all these amazing things, yet he readily admits his weaknesses, and he listens closely to his board, even though he doesn't really have to. In the hallways, he always gives you a smile. In his office, he'll think through your problem and give you fatherly encouragement about how to handle it. He's all about giving, not getting.

And money? He's mission-oriented and feels responsible to use his money to do good for others. He drives a tiny car so he can give more away, including large amounts for those in need in our community. As we on the staff work hard implementing the values he's made integral to our company, we feel great gratitude we can be part of achieving corporate goals. We're all on a mission to help fulfill the worthy goals he takes so seriously and lives out in his life.

## LEADING THE TEAM WITH DIRTY HANDS

### The Nurse Supervisor

IN A PREVIOUS CHAPTER, Melanie told the story of her nurse colleague who was promoted beyond her competence. Here she describes working under a very different supervisor who fully deserved her promotion.

Anita makes everyone on the team feel valued and appreciated. Our surgeons perform all kinds of operations, from toenail to cataract to open-heart and brain surgery. They have to have what they must have and get upset about instruments not ordered or a patient improperly prepped—any one of the countless details of an operating room. When one of them complains to Anita, she doesn't assume we messed up. She searches out the facts and defends us whenever she can.

Most of our doctors are great to work with, but their strong personalities can clash with the strong personalities of OR people. We accept the surgeons' authority, but we sometimes fume. Anita has to be

> both diplomat and problem solver while keeping everything working smoothly.
>
> She's a great boss because whether we're running the heart-lung machine or mopping the floor or carrying the anesthesia tubing, she's right there in the trenches with us, ready to grab a package of towels or find something missing. She's hands-on, a member of the team.

## EXPECTING THE BEST FROM EMPLOYEES

### The Chiropractor

HANNAH EARLIER IN the book described how negative attitudes develop even in a "warm and welcoming" office and how she dealt with her own irritability. She holds her boss in high respect and told us why her chiropractic office is a pleasant place to work:

> Doctor James may sometimes be quiet, but he's always cheerful. He'll ask, "How is your great day?" Patients feel they're with family, and they love him. We're not in a life-and-death situation but are just making patients feel better.
>
> He gives hugs, and he has a unique personality. For instance, I warn new patients that he gives people funny names, but always with a good-natured smile. He calls his wife "my lovely," and if we ask, "How's your lovely today?" he'll say, "She's drop-dead gorgeous." In our office there's a lot of positive talk about marriage—the exact opposite of some places I've worked.
>
> He's a humble guy. In the room where we do therapy and charting, he digs right in with us and

> helps. And—very important to me—Doctor James assumes the best of his employees. When he has to tell me something tough to hear he'll say, "Don't lose any sleep over this." When I had to leave suddenly because my husband had a medical emergency, unlike a previous boss, he was full of concern for us. Yet he also cares about keeping the money flowing in. He keeps tabs on insurance and how the paperwork flows. Before completing his medical degree he'd been a bread-truck driver, so he knows what work is like and what we deal with.

## INSPIRING A TOP TECH TEAM

### The Product Strategy Manager

WITH HIS DEGREE in engineering and skills in communication, Roberto has had a long and successful career in IBM and other technology companies. He travels internationally to represent his company and to troubleshoot. Here's what he says about his current boss:

> Marge admits to being obsessive/compulsive, but she never whines. There's lots of tension and jostling among the other women in the office, but she stays focused on the tasks and team building. She's collaborative. When we make client presentations together, she more than carries her end but never demands recognition. She makes it a point to share it.
>
> My boss thinks I'm great—Marge makes everyone on the team feel that way. She inspires me to work harder than I ever have in my life, and I love it!

# HIGH RESPECT FOR BOTH OWNER AND TEAM

## The Foreman

RON HAS BEEN ROOFING homes and office buildings for decades and has worked for countless bosses. He tells us the middle-aged foreman he now reports to is the best of the best. Here's what he told us about his boss:

> George is intensely focused on getting the job done, but he doesn't drive us. He shows huge respect for our eight-man crew and for the owner. The foreman before him would make disparaging remarks about the owner and gripe, but not George. His respect both ways makes for a team that loves to work together. These men come from an agency, so they seldom get respect.
>
> George doesn't just watch us work—he pitches in big time and is better at using a screw gun than anyone else. We're now working on a big K-Mart roof and because weather changes, George told us, "Any time you want to work, go to work." Now that's trust! Last week I went with my heat gun to do some sealing for a couple days, and on Monday I plan to make sure he's okay with that. We have to work to maintain trust.
>
> Our whole crew is upbeat. One of the guys fell off the roof last week and got hurt. The card everybody signed for him showed how we all felt—high respect, appreciation, and trust for each other, and George keeps making that possible.

# APPLYING BUSINESS PRINCIPLES TO MINISTRY

## The Second-Career Businessman

LEWIS WORKS IN a youth ministry that has often struggled with financial and management issues. Its leadership brought in a man in his forties willing to put his business aside and work with its president to stabilize the organization. Here's the way Lewis described him:

> Owen didn't need to make this change—he was successful in business. Working for ministry pay with four kids to put through college must crimp his family, but he's totally cheerful about becoming one of us.
>
> I love working for this guy. He's full of ideas and thinks outside the box, and he understands it all has to be funded or generate the needed income. He takes me with him when he explores high-level opportunities and when they develop, hands them off to me—but stays connected. He helped me hire some very strong people, and projects he's initiated have significantly lifted our ministries.
>
> Owen is deeply spiritual and vulnerable, once telling us he was sometimes bored at church but blamed himself for not coming in a spirit of worship. This man is authentic!

# "WHAT WORKED FOR ME"

## HOW REAL MANAGERS HANDLED TOUGH SITUATIONS

WHAT ARE YOU experiencing right now in your workplace? Chances are you face hefty challenges, and if some of them include toxic fumes, you might appreciate insights from managers in the trenches. So, we shared some of the most common predicaments we found in our interviews with thoughtful managers willing to share what they would do or have done in those circumstances. You might find helpful these managers' suggestions on what to do if you find yourself:

### Caught Between a Toxic Boss and Your Direct Reports

HA, THIS IS exactly my lot in life. I try every day to be the leader my staff deserves. I care about them personally and professionally, and that shows in the cohesiveness of our workgroup. I can't change my boss, so I just try to buffer my staff from his toxicity. When some of his "stuff gets through," they know where it's coming from and we just deal with it. We try not to let it get us down and it has somewhat become a joke. When I bring difficult issues to my boss's attention and offer solutions, he seldom responds, but my staff knows at least I tried. They appreciate the effort, because they know I am trying to make things better and not just ignoring it.

Being mediator and negotiator between my boss and employees is challenging. When in doubt, I try to err on the side of the employee.

I place my focus on what I have control of and show respect toward my boss. I try to lead by example in living a congruent life.

My boss is not toxic, and if he were, I'd leave. A toxic boss will only pass toxicity on, and no job is worth that.

## Betrayed by a "Friend"

WHAT HELPED ME most when my partner betrayed me was realizing how insecure he was. I saw how he just couldn't help himself. I had to keep on working with him, but I steeled myself to not let it eat at me.

If a betrayal is just one of those irritating things, I wouldn't address it, but I'd be cautious in the future. If it's serious betrayal, it may reveal unforeseen character flaws. I'd confront my friend face-to-face and tell them just what I planned to do about it.

It's important to let go of the anger toward that former friend. Take the high ground and be friendly, but don't share too many personal things. Let it be a learning experience.

Choose to forgive. At the same time, be cautious and keep interactions professional. Rebuilding the broken trust will take a change in your colleague's behavior.

## A Colleague Takes Credit for Your Ideas

I LAUGHED WHEN it happened! I really did. Here this guy was telling everybody, including me, that he had thought up my idea and the product itself. Sometimes work is absurd! But another time my boss in a big meeting gave the credit to another member of the team for something I actually did. That frosted me. But you know what? It didn't really matter. I needed to gulp and get over it.

Nowadays stealing credit happens in emails. People find it easier to deceive when not face-to-face—just read people's Facebook posts and tweets! When this happens I reply to the email, copying those who were not credited, and congratulate the entire team for their accomplishments. I list all those involved, even the credit hog. This lets the person who initially took the credit know that you know the truth, plus it gives credit where credit is due. I've been thanked for handling it this way by those who had their credit robbed, and it caused one offender to go back and apologize to her colleagues.

I tell myself this: Continue to complete your work with excellence, in humility. At the end of the day, the real story shines forth.

## Your Boss Won't Deal with Conflicts

JUST A CAUTION on this one—I thought my boss was being passive, but he was just overwhelmed.

He had no clue how to address the conflicts in our office, and he was so glad when we discussed it openly. We started working toward solutions.

In a new position, I was quickly hit by the fact tension in my department was high, but my boss chose to remain oblivious. So, I called a meeting and told my staff I'd meet with them one-on-one to hear their concerns and suggestions. The guidelines included these: The team as a whole would review the concerns and, as far as possible, decide on and implement the best solutions. Problems with coworkers would be expressed within process correction—no trashing of coworkers allowed! I asked them to take a chance on trusting me, and they did. The results were impressive. We repeated this process every two to three years and developed a strong, productive team.

When a boss is passive, ask for a private meeting and share the need for leadership to resolve the conflicts. Give specific examples of what's happening and suggestions for solutions and team-building strategies.

If your boss dislikes conflict or is unable to address it, do what you can to help. You're in a difficult situation, but try to be part of the solution, and come to terms with the fact you may not be able to solve this problem.

## A Clique Is Poisoning the Well

ABOUT HALF OUR team had negative attitudes that affected everybody. I determined I would be a positive influence in the building, no matter what. I went ahead and engaged my colleagues one-on-one to change the chemistry.

Here's what works for me: Evaluate what's going on and who is saying and doing what. Consider adjusting team assignments. Empower positive team members. Consider discipline if necessary.

## You're at the Breaking Point

I SEE TOO MANY employees who are reactive instead of proactive. Do you need to quit? Figure out a way to get it done and move on! Do you need to set boundaries or lessen your load? Be diplomatic but assertive. Life is too short to just keep on till you really do break.

If you need new employment, set aside time after work each day to seek it. During the workday, sharpen your skills that will make you a better candidate for the next position. Keep your cool and stay professional. Don't burn any bridges or make hasty decisions, because it is easiest to get a new job when you still have one. Deal with your stress with exercise and time with trusted friends.

Plan and take your vacations and long weekends. Establish and maintain a healthy life outside of work, engaging in activities you enjoy. Seek assistance even if it seems awkward.

Learn from mistakes. Think before you speak. Keep your resume updated.

## Your Boss Humiliates Your Coworkers

FOR ME, this is the ultimate red line. My boss once humiliated people who worked for me, and it made me furious. I confronted him. I eventually left the organization because of his attitudes. No boss should humiliate an employee!

If humiliation continues, address it privately with your boss. Evaluate as best you can whether your boss is genuinely toxic or this is an aberration brought on by circumstance. Bosses use humiliation to dominate. If your coworkers fear speaking up, carefully explore options with them, including taking it up the chain of command. There's strength in numbers. And if worse comes to worst—move on.

# CONCLUDING REMARKS

WE KNOW we haven't given you all the answers to the difficult situations you face at work. We can't. In reality, there are no easy answers. Life, work, and relationships are complicated and difficult.

But we do hope you now have a better understanding of what makes toxic workplaces the nasty places they are, and you have some gained some clarity in how to think about your situation and work relationships. (The fog typically won't go away all at once; usually it is a process that occurs over time and as a result of taking initial steps.)

We are learning more ourselves all the time. As a result, we are continuing to create resources to help you figure out how bad (or not) your situation is, whether your boss is truly toxic or just incompetent, and how to decide when "enough is enough" and it is time to start looking for another job.

Go to www.appreciationatwork.com/toxicworkplaces to look for tools, articles, and videos to help you, your friends or family members learn how to rise above a toxic workplace.

Gary Chapman
Paul White
Harold Myra

# ACKNOWLEDGMENTS

WE ARE INDEBTED to the many leaders and workers who took the time to tell us their stories. Their insights—and their honesty—informed and inspired us.

We are also indebted to our publishing team, especially John Hinkley, Zack Williamson, and Betsey Newenhuyse, for their commitment to this project and their care and creativity in helping to make it a reality.

# ABOUT THE AUTHORS

**DR. GARY CHAPMAN,** one of America's most popular relationship experts, is author of the #1 *New York Times* bestseller *The 5 Love Languages* and numerous other books. He travels the world presenting seminars. Find out more at 5lovelanguages.com.

**DR. PAUL WHITE** is a psychologist, author, and speaker who makes "work relationships work." He has consulted with a wide variety of organizations including Microsoft, NASA, the Million Dollar Round Table, Princeton University, and many more. He and Gary Chapman coauthored *The 5 Languages of Appreciation in the Workplace*. See appreciationatwork.com for more information.

**HAROLD MYRA** has written more than two dozen fiction and nonfiction books, including *The Leadership Secrets of Billy Graham*. During his thirty-two years as CEO of a magazine publishing company, the organization grew from one magazine to thirteen while establishing a thriving Internet site.